GW00383782

Emulation Ritual

Presented by

_____

To _____

Date _____

Initiated _____

Passed _____

Raised _____

Emulation
Ritual

London

LEWIS MASONIC

As demonstrated at the Emulation Lodge of Improvement, London and with whose approval this ritual has been compiled and published.

© 1980

Published by
A Lewis (Masonic Publishers) Ltd
Terminal House, Shepperton, Surrey,
who are members of the Ian Allan
Group, and printed by Ian Allan
Printing Ltd at their works at
Coombelands in Runnymede,
England.

ISBN 085318 116 0

First published 1969
Sixth and revised edition 1980

CONTENTS
EMULATION WORKING

5

CONTENTS OF APPENDIX

The contents in the following Appendix are **not** part of the Emulation working demonstrated by the Emulation Lodge of Improvement (see Preface).

Contents

PREFACE
to the Sixth Edition

With the need for the complete resetting of the type for the Emulation Ritual Book, the opportunity has been taken to make any revisions in the rubric which use has shown to be necessary. These are relatively few in number and are concerned with making completely clear, so far as is possible, the working of the ritual as practised at the Emulation Lodge of Improvement. The Notes on Ritual and Procedure have been completely revised and rearranged. In the revisions made, the Committee has made no change in the ritual wording or in the actual practice.

It may well be thought that our ritual procedures should, periodically, be brought up to date, but this poses the question as to whom licence is to be given to make alterations when the original approval came from Grand Lodge — even if it is not certain what, precisely, was approved. For this reason the Committee considers that, as a matter of trust, it should maintain without alteration, subject to decisions of Grand Lodge, the complete ritual forms handed down to it by its predecessors.

I would like to reiterate that the book is compiled and sponsored by the Committee of the Emulation Lodge of Improvement to provide an authentic record of the Emulation Ritual, and although it is intended to be useful to officers learning the work, it can in no sense take the place of attendance at Lodge of Instruction where the procedures can be thoroughly rehearsed.

The Committee wishes to thank all those who, over the ten years that this sponsored Ritual Book has been published, have commented on it and, wherever practical, the suggestions made have been implemented. The fact that the fifth edition is now exhausted demonstrates that there is still a need for the book and the Committee is happy to present this new edition in its revised form.

The Committee wishes to stress again that it is concerned with a book which sets out Emulation Working and that alone. The *Appendix* contains a number of additional and alternative forms which may be found useful; they are included by arrangement with the publishers but are not in any way a part of the Emulation Working for which the Committee is responsible.

Alan S. Trapnell   SGD
Senior Member of the Committee of the Emulation Lodge of Improvement

Members of the Committee of the Emulation Lodge of Improvement in September 1979.

RW Bro Dr A. S. Hollins, OBE, Prov Gd Master for Middlesex, *Treasurer*

W Bro His Honour Judge A. S. Trapnell, SGD, *Senior Member*
W Bro C. F. W. Dyer, ERD, PJGD, *Joint Secretary*
W Bro H. J. B. Essex, PPDGSwdB (Surrey)
W Bro N. D. Ouvry, PSGD
W Bro J. D. H. Shearman, PM 3680, *Joint Secretary*
W Bro R. C. Marley, LGR
W Bro H. M. Sharp, PGStwd

W Bro J. E. Brereton, PM 5254, *Asst Secretary*

NOTES ON RITUAL AND PROCEDURE

EMULATION Working takes its name from the Emulation Lodge of Improvement whose Committee is the custodian of this particular ritual and by whose authority this ritual book is published. The Lodge of Improvement meets at Freemasons' Hall, Gt Queen Street, London, weekly on Fridays from October to June and demonstrates the ceremonies and lectures according to Emulation working.

The Emulation Lodge of Improvement for Master Masons, to give it its full title, first met on 2 October 1823. It was formed specifically for Master Masons so as to provide instruction for those who wished to make themselves ready for Lodge office and succession to the Chair. The founders came principally from the Burlington and Perseverance Lodges of Instruction, the first formed in 1810 and the other in 1817, both of whom had taught the

11

new ritual approved by Grand Lodge in
June 1816 but who tended to concentrate
on the work of the First Degree and to
instruct candidates.

The instruction in the early years was
entirely by means of the masonic lectures
according to the system of the Grand
Stewards Lodge, which lectures describe
the ceremonies in detail. By the 1830s, in
accordance with general practice which had
then grown up, the ceremonies themselves
were also being rehearsed. The Lodge of
Improvement has met uninterruptedly since
its formation and has always had the
reputation of resistance to unauthorised
and inadvertent change in the ceremonies.

The ritual forms for use in the new
United Grand Lodge of England, as
demonstrated by the Lodge of
Reconciliation specially formed to produce
those forms, were 'approved and confirmed'
by Grand Lodge in June 1816. There have
been occasional adjustments of a ritual
nature approved by Grand Lodge since
1816, the most notable being the variations
in obligations permitted by a resolution of

Grand Lodge in December 1964 along with the consequential adjustments relating to them.

Objects of Emulation

Those responsible for the conducting of Emulation Lodge of Improvement have, from its earliest days, taken the view that their duty was to ensure the practice of an approved Ritual form without permitting alteration. While no claim could possibly be made that the present Emulation Ritual is in the exact verbal form practised one hundred and fifty years ago, the Ceremonies for use in those days had been specifically approved by Grand Lodge. This seems to the Committee to place the authority for deliberate alteration with Grand Lodge alone. It may well be thought that our ritual procedures should, periodically, be brought up to date, but this poses the question as to whom licence is to be given to make alterations when the original approval came from Grand Lodge — even if it is not certain what, precisely, was approved. For this reason the

Committee considers that, as a matter of trust, it should maintain without alteration the complete Ritual forms handed down to it by its predecessors, and that it is outside its authority to make any alterations unless officially sanctioned by resolution or acceptance of Grand Lodge itself. Grand Lodge, obviously, can alter and adjust a form of ritual which derives its authority from having been originally approved by Grand Lodge.

In these days there are many other systems of working the masonic ritual and many quite senior brethren take the view that the way that they are used to carrying out the work in their own Lodges is the only correct way. Occasionally well intentioned visitors at Lodges attempt to point out errors when, in fact, Lodges are carrying out the standard practice of the Working they use. The practices contained in this book as Emulation Working are as they have been carried out at their regular demonstrations by Emulation Lodge of Improvement for very many years and officers of Lodges in which practices are questioned by visitors should point out that the practices are perfectly correct according to this working until Grand Lodge direct otherwise.

Objects of this Ritual Book

For many years after the settling of the ritual by the Lodge of Reconciliation and its approval by Grand Lodge in 1816 (followed by the settling of the Installation Ceremony in 1827), Grand Lodge took the view quite strongly that no attempt should be made to commit the ritual to print, so that in the period immediately following — and possibly for nearly half a century — oral repetition was for many the means of learning. The Emulation weekly meetings, among others, provided the opportunity. Some printed and manuscript rituals certainly did make an appearance, though from the differences between them it is likely that they were not completely accurate, and it was not until the 1870s that printed books of ritual began to become generally accepted. Since that time a great many have been published, among which have been some purporting to set out the

Emulation system of working; but none of these has had any authorisation from the Emulation Lodge of Improvement.

It was this ban by Grand Lodge which caused Emulation to be late in the field in sponsoring publication of its own ritual, which it first did in 1969.

The compilation posed an immediate question. Should it record the system precisely as demonstrated in the Emulation Lodge of Improvement, or should its object be to provide guidance to Private Lodges? The question stems from the fact that the Emulation Lodge of Improvement is for, and can be attended by, Master Masons only, whereas Private Lodges must consider the presence of Entered Apprentices and Fellow Crafts. This contributes to certain differences in procedure. An example is that in the Emulation Lodge of Improvement the Master does not request EAs or FCs to retire before the Lodge is opened in the next higher degree. None can be present, so the request would be pointless; but it is quite proper in a Private Lodge.

In presenting the book, it has been a primary concern of the Committee that it should provide as much assistance as possible to Officers of Lodges whose procedure is based on Emulation, but neither this book nor any other can ever be a substitute for organised rehearsal and attendance at Lodge of Instruction, as it is there that what is set out in this book is brought to life.

Layout of Lodge Rooms

The Emulation Ritual is based on the form of Lodge layout found in the Lodge Rooms at Freemasons' Hall, Great Queen Street, London. As these Rooms are maintained under the direct control of Grand Lodge administration it is felt that this is the standard layout for English masonry when the circumstances of meeting places make it possible for it to be followed. In these Lodge Rooms the chequered carpet covers the whole of the centre of the Lodge Room and the three pedestals are so placed that they are just off the carpet in the E, S and W. In order to approach the Master and Wardens in their pedestals, as in the case of perambulations, entrustings and testings, it is therefore necessary, in order to work the Emulation system correctly, to go off the carpet and stand alongside the pedestals. Thus, because of the position of the carpet covering the whole floor, all perambulations are actually carried out on the carpet except when the Can is taken to the pedestals of the Master and Wardens. References to the Can being taken on to 'the floor of the Lodge' means that he is taken on the carpet itself, usually for the purpose of perambulation.

Similarly, the doors to the Lodge rooms are at the west end of the Lodge, to the north of the IG's seat in most cases, making it simple for the IG to carry out his duties from his normal seat on the north of the SW. The SD's chair is placed at the east end of the north column facing directly across the Lodge (and not across the corner) — although in the Emulation Lodge of Improvement's demonstrations the SD is placed in his older position at the right hand of the WM, facing down the

Lodge, a seat now normally occupied by the senior Grand Officer. The JD's chair is on the south side of the SW facing squarely up the Lodge (again, not across the corner).

Where circumstances of Lodge rooms and size of carpet make some of these conditions impossible, Lodges wishing to work to the Emulation system will have no difficulty in getting as closely as possible to the layout and using the full extent of the open area between the WM and Wardens, etc, for perambulations. Where differences in Lodge layout and the nature of the Lodge of Improvement demonstrations may cause some difficulty in following exactly the work as demonstrated at Emulation Lodge of Improvement, an asterisk* in the text indicates that some help may be found in these Notes.

The Appendix

It is the Ritual and Procedure during the four basic ceremonies with the necessary adjuncts such as openings and closings which are the concern of the Emulation Committee and it does not presume to lay down any standards of procedure outside of this. It will, however, be appreciated that merely to print the four ceremonies with the openings and closings would not make a complete work. Arrangements have therefore been made with the Publishers to include an Appendix of matters which, although outside the scope of 'Emulation' may be of assistance to members of the Craft generally, but its contents are not in any way a part of the Emulation Working as demonstrated at the regular meetings of the Emulation Lodge of Improvement.

Punctuation

There is no doubt that, in certain places, the words used are capable of being given more than one shade of meaning, while the phrasing may cause difficulty to the average Lodge officer. Where there is room for difference of opinion on punctuation therefore, two main objectives have been kept in mind; (1) to ensure that the sense which the Committee believes to be intended is made plain, and (2) to give assistance to the Lodge officer with his phrasing. It is not anticipated that opinion will be unanimous about the result, particularly as the Committee feels that punctuation can, so very often, be a matter of personal preference and, also, may be the outcome of changes in fashion.

Type Setting

In this book an Officer's designation is shown in **bold type** if he is required to speak or take other action. The printing in Roman type indicates that words are spoken, while that in *italic* type is descriptive of an action or is used by way of explanation.

Some Lodges use the Permissive Alternative forms of Obligation sanctioned by Grand Lodge in 1964. To allow for these and for the necessary consequential adjustments, the traditional form is indicated by a single vertical line in the left margin followed by the alternative form indicated by a double vertical line.

General Ritual Notes

The Emulation Lodge of Improvement having been set up as a Master Masons' Lodge, it has always been and still is today opened straightway in the Three Degrees, and the Brethren do not sit between the various opening ceremonies. The Lodge of Improvement is then resumed as may be necessary in the appropriate degree for the work or business to be done, and at the end of the proceedings, after being resumed in the Third Degree if necessary, the Lodge is closed in the Three Degrees in full. However, when the Installation Ceremony is worked, the Lodge is closed in the normal way in the Third and Second Degrees during that Ceremony. Being a Master Masons' Lodge the business of the Lodge is conducted in the Third Degree, again with the exception of the business on the Risings after the Installation Ceremony which are taken in the First Degree. A regular Lodge may have EAs and FCs among its members so that business is normally transacted in the First Degree to enable all members to participate.

As already mentioned no provision needs to be made at Emulation demonstrations for the retirement of EAs and FCs nor for Emergency meetings and in these and other instances suitable procedures are suggested for the sake of continuity.

Obligations in Ceremonies

The original meaning, spelling and pronunciation of the word immediately preceding the words "conceal and never reveal" is uncertain. In the Lodge of Improvement what it believes to be the original pronunciation is maintained and therefore in this book the word is shown as "h (*pronounced hail*)".

Master's Work

In the Emulation Lodge of Improvement the whole of the Chair work is demonstrated by the WM (or IM) and this book follows that practice. In those Lodges were a Chaplain is one of the Officers, prayers are normally said by him. In many Lodges parts of the Degree Ceremonies are often worked by brethren other than the

WM, but it is felt that such work should not normally be undertaken by other than Installed Masters or Wardens. When work is undertaken by brethren other than the WM, it is considered that all the officers should follow the usual procedure as if the WM were doing the work.

Organ and SMIB

No organ is used in Emulation Lodge of Improvement and SMIB is said only by the Committee member acting as PM; this book sets out that practice. Many Lodges use an organ and music is a normal part of the proceedings; opening and closing odes may be sung and SMIB chanted by all present.

The VSL

At Emulation Lodge of Improvement the VSL is opened on the WM's pedestal so that the print is placed for him to read and the Sq and Cs normally on the r h page as the WM looks at it. The pt of the Sq and the pts of the Cs are towards the bottom of the page and towards the WM.

Openings and Closings

In many Lodges there is a procession into Lodge. This is entirely a matter for the Lodge to decide.

In the First Degree opening, the question asked by the WM 'The Master's place?' in Emulation Lodge of Improvement is addressed to the SW. In some Lodges it is asked of the IPM.

On all occasions when the JW addresses the WM he faces directly across the Lodge to his front, turning only his head and not his body towards the WM.

When the IG addresses the JW, he, similarly, faces directly to his front (towards the WM) and turns his head only towards the JW. When addressing either the JW or the WM, the position of the IG should be immediately in front of his chair.

At the opening and closing of the Lodge in the various Degrees and when resuming labour from one Degree to another, the ks of the WM, the Wardens and the IG and Tyler are given in sequence without waiting for any other action to take place. At Emulation Lodge of Improvement the adjustments of the VSL and the Sq and Cs are done informally while the ks are progressing and not at any particular moment between any ks. The IPM adjusts them in his own time after the appropriate declaration has been made, doing so from his position on the left of the WM.

Tracing Boards

As only Master Masons are admitted to the Emulation Lodge of Improvement, the changing of the Tracing Boards has no significance, and there is at our demonstrations no procedure for carrying this out. Our practice is for that Tracing Board to be displayed on the floor of the Lodge which is appropriate to the Degree being demonstrated and for the Installation ceremony no Board is displayed. The Tracing Boards are in any case too large and heayy to permit of easy handling, so that the Boards are changed during an interval when the Lodge is Called Off. The Tracing Boards of the Lodge of Improvement were designed and made in 1845 before it became common practice to display and change Boards on changing Degrees in which the Lodge is open. When sections of a Lecture are worked, the Tracing Board appropriate to the Degree of the Lecture is displayed. In a Regular Lodge where the changing of the Boards is usual, the text provides for the Tracing Boards to be attended to at appropriate times in accordance with the normal practice of the Lodge.

If Lodges do change Tracing Boards at the opening and closing in the various Degrees, it is suggested that the Deacon moves to make the change immediately the JW has gavelled and that the IG does not wait for the Boards to be changed before going to the door to give the ks.

No one but the IG should open or close the door at any time and the IG should retain control of the door while remaining within the entrance.

Deacons' Work

The method of holding the Can, especially in the Initiation Ceremony, is a matter not of ritual but of common sense.

Interlacing the fingers is often the best, except when Can and D are of a disparate height when it may be found more convenient to grasp firmly the Can's wrist. The Ds arm should be behind the Can's, the elbow kept fairly rigid, and the shoulder tucked slightly behind the Can's. Such linking enables the D easily to urge forward or restrain the Can, or to change his direction. When the Can is h...w...d, his hand is always held except when he is kneeling. At other times the D holds the Can's h only when they are actually moving from one place to another; when D and Can are stationary, the Can's h is released.

When the Can is at the WM's ped for Obl and entrusting, he is in the hands of the WM. The D should not volunteer assistance unless it is clear that the WM really needs it, and even then the assistance should be as unobtrusive as possible.

D and Can should stand square at the W's peds. In Emulation demonstrations the deacons carry wands during the ritual ceremonies but not during business procedure such as ballots, etc.

When the Can is about to take his Obl in the First Degree, the WM should be careful not to gavel heavily. This could cause the Can to give a start and so injure himself. A further safeguard is to ensure that the Can grasps the Cs in a way which cannot put pressure on the pt.

Standing to Order in Third Degree

In the Third Degree, for the Obl, for addressing the WM, for closing and in other places the Brethren are required to stand to order with Sp and MM P Sn. The static position for the P Sn where this has to be done is slightly different from the position illustrated to the Can as shown on page 185. When standing to order in the degree the r h is placed straight away w t t t n and held there. In dis the Sn the h is first taken to t l o t b and the Sn completed as described on page 185.

Third Degree G or T

The G in the Third Degree both for entrusting and in the closing is given by the th and f f of each Bro encircling as far as possible the b of the th of the other. This will bring the f f on to one side of the w, the remaining fs are placed on the other side of the w so that the w is spanned between the f f and m f.

The Installation Ceremony

The presentation of the Master Elect at Emulation Lodge of Improvement demonstrations is by a Committee member acting as PM, while the Installing Master conducts the entire proceedings. The demonstrations were commenced before the custom of appointing Lodge DCs. In these days in most Lodges a great deal of work is done by the Lodge DC at Installations and in the text this is indicated by '(*or* **DC**)' at the appropriate places.

Also at Emulation demonstrations the Installed Masters who are to act as Wardens to make up the Board are placed in their chairs in the Third Degree, because this is the working Degree for Emulation Lodge of Improvement as a Master

Masons' Lodge. The Committee believes that this filling of the Wardens' chairs was meant to be done in Lodges in the First Degree, after the EAs have retired and immediately before the raising of the Lodge to the Second Degree, when the ME is presented.

The new WM remains seated at Emulation demonstrations when the IM presents to him the Warrant.

The Tyler, when admitted for investing, goes unaccompanied, after saluting, to the WM's ped in the course of our demonstrations. It is appreciated that in many Lodges he is conducted by the DC.

The Tyler, on arrival at the WM's ped, lays his Swd diagonally across the VSL where it remains while he is invested and until the WM hands it back to him. Many masons object to this practice, which appears not to be done in other workings, but the Committee does not subscribe to these objections. They see no harm in a practice which has been part of Emulation Ritual since the 1830s and which is performed with both ceremony and reverence. Lodges in which this practice nevertheless gives offence will no doubt obey the dictates of their own conscience.

Greetings (Salutes)

Greetings accorded to the WM during the Installation ceremony are given audibly.

For the Third Degree G or R S, the first movement of the hs is upwards to a point over or just in front of the head. When used as a greeting, it begins with an overhead clap of the hs, not a preliminary slap of the thighs.

Working Tools

The explanation of working tools in any Degree is not given twice in the same evening. When this might occur because of a Degree ceremony as well as Installation a form of words is used to the effect that they have been previously explained.

By-laws

The wording of the Installation ceremony contains a recommendation to the new Master that the By-laws of the Lodge should be read at least once in the year and such a recommendation has appeared in the ceremony for a very long time. There is no requirement in the Book of Constitutions that By-laws be read in Lodge and the Board of General Purposes has indicated that, as all members must have a copy of them, there is no need for such a reading in Lodge.

Calling Off and On

At any time when it is desired to have a general break in the Lodge proceedings and for the brethren to leave the Lodge room, a formal 'calling off' by the use of the ritual procedure shown on page 60 should be used. The Lodge should be formally 'called on' by the procedure on page 61 before the Lodge business is continued.

Attention is called to the Report of the Board of General Purposes of 8 March 1961 on page eight of the Points of Procedure, requiring the Lodge to be properly called off if a break is made.

Ballots

The method of balloting observed in

B

the Lodge of Improvement is by the use of a two-drawer ballot box. The JD distributes the tokens, starting with the PM and finishing with the WM. The SD presents the box to the WM on the S side for proof of its being clear and then collects the tokens in the same sequence as the JD on distribution, collecting the WM's from the N side of the pedestal, then proceeding to the S side for the examination and announcement of the result. The SD remains at S side of the WM's pedestal until after the announcement.

Entry of Latecomers and Candidates

At the Emulation Lodge of Improvement, the Tyler gives the ks of the Degree in which the Lodge is open in order to announce latecomers. The IG, at a convenient time, announces the report to the JW who replies with one k. Having ascertained the reason for the report, the IG announces to the WM a latecomer by name only (that is, he does NOT add 'seeks admission' or other similar form of words). If there is more than one brother, the IG's announcement would be 'WM, Bro ....., and other brethren'. The WM having ordered their admission, the IG lets them in and they go to the l (or north) of the SW's ped, giving, in sequence, the sns of all the Degrees up to that in which the Lodge is open. Having thus saluted, they go to seats.

For a Can, the Tyler's ks are those of the highest Degree the Can has received and should be given as soon as the Tyler has the Can ready. The WM can decide when it is suitable for the IG to give a report. It is preferable for the Can's ks to be clearly given and, in the First Degree, to be three distinct ks — at longer intervals than the normal ks of the Degree.

OPENING

The Brethren assemble in their places. An opening ode may be sung.

WM *one* ━▙ **SW** *one* ━▙ **JW** *one* ━▙

WM — Brethren, assist me to open the Lodge.

ALL *rise (if not already standing after opening ode).*

WM *names JW* — Bro ......, what is the first care of every Mason?

JW — To see that the Lodge is properly tyled.

WM — Direct that duty to be done.

JW *names IG* — Bro ......, see that the Lodge is properly tyled.

IG *goes to door, does not open it, gives three distinct ks and returns to position in front of his chair.**

Tyler *responds with same ks.*

IG, *no Sp or Sn, names JW* — Bro ......, the Lodge is properly tyled.

JW *three distinct* ━▙ *no Sp or Sn, to*

See Notes on Ritual and Procedure.

WM, no name — The Lodge is properly tyled.

WM *names SW* — Bro ......, the next care?

SW — To see that none but Masons are present.

WM — To order Brethren in the First Degree.

ALL *take Sp, with EA Sn.*

WM — Bro JW, how many principal officers are there in the Lodge?

JW — Three: the WM, and the S and J Ws.

WM — Bro SW, how many assistant officers are there?

SW — Three, besides the T or OG: namely, the S and JDs, and the IG.

WM *to JW* — The situation of the T?

JW — Outside the door of the Lodge.

WM — His duty?

JW — Being armed with a drawn sword to keep off all intruders and cowans to Masonry and to see that the Candidates are properly prepared.

WM *to SW* — The situation of the IG?

SW — Within the entrance of the Lodge.

WM — His duty?

SW — To admit Masons on proof, receive the Candidates in due form, and obey the commands of the JW.

WM *to JW* — The situation of the JD?

JW — At the right of the SW.

WM — His duty?

JW — To carry all messages and communications of the WM from the S to the JW, and to see that the same are punctually obeyed.

WM *to SW* — The situation of the SD?

SW — At or near to the right of the WM.

WM — His duty?

SW — To bear all messages and commands from the WM to the SW, and await the return of the JD.

WM — Bro JW, your place in the Lodge?

JW — In the S.

WM — Why are you placed there?

JW — To mark the sun at its meridian, to call the Brethren from labour to refreshment and from refreshment to labour, that profit and pleasure may be the result.

WM — Bro SW, your place in the Lodge?

SW — In the W.

WM — Why are you placed there?

SW — To mark the setting sun, to close the Lodge by command of the WM, after having seen that every Brother has had his due.

*WM *to SW* — The Master's place?

SW — In the E.

WM — Why is he placed there?

SW — As the sun rises in the E to open and enliven the day, so the WM is placed in the E to open the Lodge, and employ and instruct the Brethren in Freemasonry.

*WM — The Lodge being duly formed, before I declare it open, let us invoke the assistance of the Great Architect of the Universe in all our undertakings; may our labours, thus begun in order, be conducted in peace, and closed in harmony.

*IPM — So mote it be.

WM — Brethren, in the name of the Great Architect of the Universe, I declare the Lodge duly open (**ALL** *cut Sn*) for the

*See Notes on Ritual and Procedure.

purposes of Freemasonry in the First Degree.

WM — *EA* ⊢

SW — *EA* ⊢ *and raises Cn.*

JW — *EA* ⊢ *and lowers Cn.*

TB is attended to when JW has given ks. (In EL of Imp the TBs are not changed: in Lodges it is usually done by* **JD.)

IG *goes to door, gives EA ks and returns to position in front of his chair.*

Tyler *responds with same ks.*

IPM, *meanwhile, opens VSL and arranges Sq and Cs. (In EL of Imp this is done from IPM's position at S of WM.)*

VSL is placed so that WM can read it: pts of the Cs are directed to WM and hidden by the arms of the Sq, angle towards WM.

***WM** *sits when this has been completed.*

***ALL** *the brethren take their seats when the WM sits.*

**See Notes on Ritual and Procedure.*

OPENING IN THE SECOND DEGREE

Before opening in the Second Degree **WM** *would normally request EAs to retire.*

WM *one* ━�ً **SW** *one* ━▌ **JW** *one* ━▌.

WM — Brethren, assist me to open the Lodge in the Second Degree.

*ALL rise, if not already standing.

WM — Bro JW, what is the first care of every FC FM?

JW — To see that the Lodge is properly tyled.

WM — Direct that duty to be done.

JW — Bro IG, see that the Lodge is properly tyled.

IG *goes to door, gives EA ks and returns to position in front of his chair.**

Tyler *responds with same ks.*

IG *Sp and EA Sn* — Bro JW, the Lodge is properly tyled — *cuts Sn.*

JW *EA* ━▌, *Sp and EA Sn* — WM, the Lodge is properly tyled — *cuts Sn.*

*See Notes on Ritual and Procedure.

WM — Bro SW, the next care?

SW — To see that the Brethren appear to order as Masons.

WM — To order, Brethren, in the First Degree.

ALL *take Sp, with EA Sn.*

WM — Bro JW, are you a FC FM?

JW — I am, WM, try me and prove me.

WM — By what instrument in architecture will you be proved?

JW — The S.

WM — What is a S?

JW — An angle of 90 Degrees, or the fourth part of a Circle.

WM — Being yourself acquainted with the proper method, you will prove the Brethren Craftsmen, and demonstrate that proof to me by copying their example.

JW — Brethren, it is the WM's command that you prove yourselves Craftsmen.

ALL *(except WM and JW) cut EA Sn, take Sp with FC Sn.*

JW *having assured himself that all have proved themselves* — WM, the Brethren have proved themselves Craftsmen, and in obedience to your command I thus copy their example — *cuts EA Sn; Sp and FC Sn.*

WM — Bro JW I acknowledge the correctness of the Sn — *cuts EA Sn; Sp and FC Sn.*

*WM — Before we open the Lodge in the Second Degree, let us supplicate the Grand Geometrician of the Universe, that the rays of Heaven may shed their influence to enlighten us in the paths of virtue and science.

*IPM — So mote it be.

WM — Brethren, in the name of the Grand Geometrician of the Universe, I declare the Lodge duly open (**ALL** *cut Sn*) on the Sq, for the instruction and improvement of Craftsmen.

WM — *FC* ➞ **SW** — *FC* ➞ **JW** — *FC* ➞.

* TB is attended to when JW has given ks (usually by **JD**).

IG *goes to the door, gives FC ks and returns to position in front of his chair.**

Tyler *responds with same ks.*

*See Notes on Ritual and Procedure.

IPM, *meanwhile, exposes one p of Cs.*
*WM *sits when this has been completed.*
*ALL *sit.*

OPENING IN THE THIRD DEGREE

**Before opening in the Third Degree*
WM *would normally request FCs to retire.*

WM *one* ➔ **SW** *one* ➔ **JW** *one*
➔.

WM — Brethren, assist me to open the Lodge in the Third Degree.

*ALL *rise, if not already standing.*

WM — Bro JW, what is the first care of every MM?

JW — To see that the Lodge is properly tyled.

WM — Direct that duty to be done.

JW — Bro IG, see that the Lodge is properly tyled.

IG *goes to door, gives FC ks and returns to position in front of his chair.***

Tyler *responds with same ks.*

IG *Sp and FC Sn* — Bro JW, the Lodge

*See Notes on Ritual and Procedure.

is properly tyled — *cuts Sn.*

JW *FC* ➡️**⌐**, *Sp and FC Sn.* WM, the lodge is properly tyled — *cuts Sn.*

WM — Bro SW, the next care?

SW — To see that the Brethren appear to order as Craftsmen.

WM — To order, Brethren, in the Second Degree.

ALL *take Sp with FC Sn.*

WM — Bro JW, are you a MM?

JW — I am, WM, try me and prove me.

WM — By what instruments in Architecture will you be proved?

JW — The S and Cs

WM — Being yourself acquainted with the proper method, you will prove the Brethren MMs by Sns and demonstrate that proof to me by copying their example.

JW — Brethren, it is the WM's command that you prove yourselves MMs by Sns.

ALL *except* **WM** *and* **JW** *take Sp, give S of H, S of S and P Sn to point of recovery, holding Sn.*

JW — WM, the Brethren have proved themselves MMs by Sns, and in obedience

to your command I thus copy their example
*—takes Sp and gives the three Sns holding
P Sn at point of recovery.*

WM — Bro JW, I acknowledge the
correctness of the Sns — *takes Sp and
gives the three Sns holding P Sn at point of
recovery.*

WM — Bro JW, whence come you?

JW — The E.

WM — Bro SW, whither directing your
course?

SW — The W.

WM *to JW* — What inducement have
you to leave the E and go to the W?

JW — To seek for that which was lost,
which, by your instruction and our own
industry, we hope to find.

WM *to SW* — What is that which was
lost?

SW — The genuine secrets of a MM.

WM *to JW* — How came they lost?

JW — By the untimely death of our M,
H A.

WM *to SW* — Where do you hope to
find them?

SW — With the C.

WM *to JW* — What is a C?

JW — A point within a circle, from which every part of the circumference is equidistant.

WM *to SW* — Why with the C?

SW — That being a point from which a MM cannot err.

*WM — We will assist you to repair that loss and may Heaven aid our united endeavours.

*IPM — So mote it be.

WM — Brethren, in the name of the Most High, I declare the Lodge duly open (**ALL** *cut Sn, no re-recovery*), on the C, for the purposes of Freemasonry in the Third Degree.

WM *MM* ➡️ **SW** *MM* ➡️ **JW** *MM* ➡️.

TB is attended to when JW has given ks (usually by **JD**).

IG *goes to door, gives MM ks and returns to position in front of his chair.**

Tyler *responds with same ks.*

IPM, *meanwhile, exposes both pts of Cs. Any who have relaxed it, retake Sp.*

*See Notes on Ritual and Procedure.

WM — All Glory to the Most High.
ALL *give G or R Sn.*
WM *sits.*
ALL *sit.*

CLOSING IN THE THIRD DEGREE

WM *one* ▬▬❙ **SW** *one* ▬▬❙ **JW** *one* ▬▬❙.

WM — Brethren, assist me to close the Lodge in the Third Degree.

ALL *rise.*

WM — Bro JW , what is the constant care of every MM?

JW — To prove the Lodge close tyled.

WM — Direct that duty to be done.

JW — Bro IG, prove the Lodge close tyled.

IG *goes to door, gives MM ks and returns to position in front of his chair.***

Tyler *responds with same ks.*

IG *Sp and P Sn of MM* — Bro JW the Lodge is close tyled — *completes Sn to recovery and drops hand.*

*See Notes on Ritual and Procedure.

JW *MM* ━┫, *Sp and P Sn of MM*
WM, the Lodge is close tyled — *completes
Sn to recovery and drops hand.*

WM — Bro SW, the next care?

SW — To see that the Brethren appear
to order as MMs.

WM — To order, Brethren, in the Third
Degree.

ALL *take Sp with P Sn of MM.*

WM — Bro JW, whence come you?

JW — The W, whither we have been in
search of the genuine Scts of a MM.

WM — Bro SW, have you found them?

SW — We have not, WM, but we bring
with us certain substituted Scts, which we
are anxious to impart for your approbation.

WM — Let those substituted Scts be
regularly communicated to me.

SW *holding P Sn of MM leaves ped by N
side and proceeds E, keeping to N of centre
line of Lodge until he reaches a convenient
point just past JW's ped where he turns
inwards to face S and stands with Sp and
Sn.*

JW *holding P Sn of MM leaves ped by W
side at convenient moment to proceed E in*

line with *SW* keeping to *S* of centre line of
Lodge until *SW* turns inwards and halts
with *Sp* and *Sn*; *JW* then turns inwards to
face *SW*, halting with *Sp* and *Sn* a
convenient distance from him.

JW takes further *Sp*, holds out *r h* to
SW and taking his *r h* communicates *pg*
leading from Second to Third Degree,
raises hands head high and communicates *pw* in a whisper. Hands are released
and *JW* resumes *Sn*.

SW resumes *Sn*.

JW takes further *Sp*, gives *S of H*, *S of S*
and *P Sn* to recovery. *JW* then
communicates *F P O F* and whispers *wds* of
a *MM*; on completion he resumes position
holding *Sp* of *P Sn*.

SW follows *JW*, receiving *F P O F*, and
after communication of words, resumes
position holding *Sp* and *P Sn*.

JW salutes *SW* with *P Sn* to recovery
and holding it returns to *ped* with *Sp*.

SW holding *Sn* turns on centre line of
Lodge to *WM* and with *Sp* — **WM**,
condescend to receive from me the
substituted Scts of a MM.

WM — Bro SW, I will receive them with pleasure, and for the information of the Brethren you will speak the words aloud — *leaves ped by S side still holding Sn and faces SW with Sp at a convenient distance.*

SW *takes Sp, holds out r h to WM and taking his r h with p g, raises hands head high and communicates p w aloud. Hands are released and SW resumes Sn.*

WM *takes SW's r h at appropriate moment and on release of hands resumes Sn.*

SW *takes further Sp gives S of H, S of S and P Sn to recovery. He then communicates F P O F and, aloud, wds of a MM, and on completion resumes position holding Sp and P Sn.*

WM *follows SW receiving F P O F and after communicating wds, resumes position holding Sp and P Sn.*

SW *salutes WM with P Sn to recovery and holding it returns to ped with Sp.*

WM, *after salute, at the same time returns to ped with Sp and holding Sn.*

WM — Brethren, the substituted Scts of a MM, thus regularly communicated to me,

I, as M of this Lodge, and thereby the humble representative of KS, sanction and confirm with my approbation, and declare that they shall designate you, and all MMs throughout the Universe, until time or circumstance shall restore the genuine.

ALL *bend a little forward* — With gratitude to our Master we bend.

WM — All gratitude to the Most High.

ALL give G of R Sn and then resume P Sn.

WM — Bro SW, the labours of this Degree being ended, you have my command to close the Lodge — MM ➤ *(with l h)*.

SW — Brethren, in the name of the Most High and by command of the WM, I close (**ALL** *complete Sn to recovery and drop hands*) this MM's Lodge — MM ➤ .

JW — And it is closed accordingly — MM ➤ .

*TB is attended to when JW has given ks (usually by **JD**).

IG *goes to door, gives MM ks and*

See Notes on Ritual and Procedure.

*returns to position in front of his chair.**

Tyler *responds with same ks.*

IPM, *meanwhile, conceals one pt of Cs under S.**

***WM** sits when this has been completed.*
***ALL** sit.*

CLOSING IN THE SECOND DEGREE

WM *one* ▬▬▬ **SW** *one* ▬▬▬ **JW** *one* ▬▬▬.

WM — Brethren, assist me to close the Lodge in the Second Degree.

***ALL** rise if not already standing.*

WM — Bro JW, what is the constant care of every FC FM?

JW — To prove the Lodge close tyled.

WM — Direct that duty to be done.

JW — Bro IG, prove the Lodge close tyled.

IG *goes to door, gives FC ks and returns to position in front of his chair.**

See Notes on Ritual and Procedure.

Tyler *responds with same ks.*

IG *Sp and FC Sn* — Bro JW, the Lodge is close tyled — *cuts Sn.*

JW *FC* ▬▬ , *Sp and FC Sn* — WM, the Lodge is close tyled — *cuts Sn.*

WM — Bro SW, the next care?

SW — To see that the Brethren appear to order as Craftsmen.

WM — To order, Brethren, in the Second Degree.

ALL *take Sp with FC Sn.*

WM — Bro JW, in this position, what have you discovered?

JW — A sacred Symbol.

WM — Bro SW, where is it situated?

SW — In the Centre of the building.

WM *to JW* — To whom does it allude?

JW — The Grand Geometrician of the Universe.

*WM — Then, Brethren, let us remember that wherever we are, and whatever we do, He is with us, and His all-seeing eye observes us, and whilst we continue to act in conformity with the principles of the Craft, let us not fail to discharge our duty

*See Notes on Ritual and Procedure.

to Him with fervency and zeal.

*IPM — So mote it be.

WM — Bro SW, the labours of this Degree being ended, you have my command to close the Lodge — *FC* ➤ *(with lh)*.

SW — Brethren, in the name of the Grand Geometrician of the Universe, and by command of the WM, I close **(ALL** *cut Sn)* this FC's Lodge — *FC* ➤.

JW — Happy have we met,
          Happy may we part,
          And happy meet again
— *FC* ➤.

*TB is attended to when JW has given ks (usually by **JD***).*

IG *goes to door, gives FC ks and returns to position in front of his chair.*

Tyler *responds with same ks.*

IPM, *meanwhile, conceals both pts of the Cs under the S.**

*WM sits when this has been completed.

*ALL sit.

---

*See Notes on Ritual and Procedure.

CLOSING

Before finally closing the Lodge at the end of a regular meeting, there are three risings according to the following formula:

WM *one* ━┫ **SW** *one* ━┫ **JW** *one* ━┫

WM — Brethren, I rise — *rises* — for the first (*or* second *or* third) time to ask if any Brother has aught to propose for the good of Freemasonry in general or of this (*names Lodge*) ...... in particular.

On each rising such business is transacted as is customary in the Lodge. When all business on the third rising is completed:

WM *one* ━┫ **SW** *one* ━┫ **JW** *one* ━┫

WM — Brethren, assist me to close the Lodge.

*ALL *rise, if not already standing.*

WM — Bro JW, what is the constant care of every Mason?

JW — To prove the Lodge close tyled.

*See Notes on Ritual and Procedure.

WM — Direct that duty to be done.

JW — Bro IG, prove the Lodge close tyled.

IG *goes to door, gives EA ks and returns to position in front of his chair.**

Tyler *responds with same ks.*

IG — *Sp and EA Sn* — Bro JW, the Lodge is close tyled — *cuts Sn.*

JW — *EA* ━━■ *Sp and EA Sn* — WM, the Lodge is close tyled — *cuts Sn.*

WM — Bro SW, the next care?

SW — To see that the Brethren appear to order as Masons.

WM — To order, Brethren, in the First Degree.

ALL *take Sp with EA Sn.*

WM — Bro SW, your constant place in the Lodge?

SW — In the W.

WM — Why are you placed there?

SW — As the sun sets in the W to close the day, so the SW is placed in the W to close the Lodge by command of the WM, after having seen that every Brother has had his due.

*See Notes on Ritual and Procedure.

*WM — Brethren, before we close the Lodge, let us with all reverence and humility express our gratitude to the Great Architect of the Universe for favours already received; may He continue to preserve the Order by cementing and adorning it with every moral and social virtue.

*IPM — So mote it be.

WM — Bro SW, the labours of the evening being ended, you have my command to close the Lodge — *EA*━▌ (*with l h*).

SW — Brethren, in the name of the Great Architect of the Universe, and by command of the WM, I close — **ALL** *cut Sn* — the Lodge.

SW — *EA*━▌ *and lowers Cn.*

*JW — And it is closed accordingly until ...... day of ......, emergencies excepted, of which every Brother will have due notice (*or* of which due notice will be given) — *EA* ━▌ *and raises Cn.*

* *TB is attended to when JW has given ks (usually by* **JD**).

**See Notes on Ritual and Procedure.*

IG *goes to door, gives EA ks and returns to position in front of his chair.**

Tyler *responds with same ks.*

IPM, *meanwhile, removes Sq and Cs, closes VSL and places Sq and Cs in convenient position on pedestal.**

IPM — Brethren, nothing now remains, but, according to ancient custom, to lock up our Scts, in a safe repository, uniting in the act F, F, F.

ALL *touch l b lightly with r h, with each word 'F'.*

* *In many Lodges, a closing ode is sung and a procession formed for WM to leave the Lodge Room.*

CALLING OFF

(For information when this is used, see Notes on Ritual and Procedure)

WM *one* ▬▶ **SW** *one* ▬▶ **JW** *one* ▬▶

WM — Principal officers upstanding.

WM, SW *and* **JW** *rise.*

WM — Bro JW, what time is it?

JW — High time, WM.

WM — Your duty?

JW — To call the Brethren from labour to refreshment.

WM — I will thank you to declare it.

JW — Brethren, it is the WM's command that you cease labour and go to refreshment. Keep within hail, so as to come on in due time, that profit and pleasure may be the result — *one* ▬▶ *and raises Cn.*

SW *one* ▬▶ *and lowers Cn.*

WM *one* ▬▶

IPM — *rises and closes VSL leaving Sq and Cs in position inside.*

*TB *is attended to (usually by* **JD***).*

ALL *may now rise and leave the Lodge Room.*

*See Notes on Ritual and Procedure.

CALLING ON

(For information on when this is used, see Notes on Ritual and Procedure)

ALL *reassemble in the Lodge Room, seated.*

WM *one* —❙ **SW** *one* —❙ **JW** *one* —❙

WM — Principal officers upstanding.

WM, SW *and* **JW** *rise.*

WM — Bro JW, what time is it?

JW — Past high time, WM.

WM — Your duty?

JW — To call the Brethren from refreshment to labour.

WM — I will thank you to declare it.

JW — Brethren, it is the WM's command that you cease refreshment and return to labour for the further despatch of Masonic business — *one* —❙ *and lowers Cn.*

SW *one* —❙ *and raises Cn.* **WM** *one* —❙

IPM *rises, opens VSL, checks that S and Cs are correctly positioned, and sits.*

*TB *is attended to (usually by* **JD**).

WM *sits when this is completed.*

SW *and* **JW** *sit.*

Business is proceeded with.

*See Notes on Ritual and Procedure.

RESUMING

A Lodge may be resumed, upwards or downwards, in any degree in which it has been previously opened, provided that the degree in question has not been formally closed.

WM one ➤ **SW** one ➤ **JW** one ➤ . (**ALL** *remain seated*).

WM — Brethren, by virtue of the power in me vested, I resume the Lodge in the ...... Degree — *gives ks of the Degree in which the Lodge is resumed.*

SW , ➤ *of degree in which Lodge is resumed.*

JW ➤ *of degree in which Lodge is resumed.*

TB is attended to after JW has given ks. (usually by **JD**).

IG *goes to door, gives ks of Degree in which Lodge is resumed and returns to his seat.*

Tyler *responds with same ks.*

IPM, *meanwhile, adjusts S and Cs to position for degree in which Lodge is resumed.*

*See Notes on Ritual and Procedure.

62

FIRST DEGREE
OR
CEREMONY OF INITIATION

Tyler *prepares Can and when ready to proceed with Ceremony gives three distinct ks. By giving the EA ks with longer intervals the Tyler indicates that the Can is ready.*

IG *rises in front of his chair, Sp and EA Sn* — Bro JW, there is a report — *holds Sn.*

JW *seated, also gives three distinct* ➤ *rises, Sp and EA Sn* — WM, there is a report — *holds Sn.*

WM — Bro JW, inquire who wants admission.

JW *cuts Sn and sits* — Bro IG, see who wants admission.

IG *cuts Sn and goes to door of Lodge, unlocks it, does not leave Lodge, but remains on threshold with hand on door handle, and assures himself that Can is properly prepared. (The colloquy between IG and Tyler should be spoken loud enough*

63

for it to be heard in all parts of the Lodge.)

IG, *to Tyler* — Whom have you there?

T *names Can* — Mr ......, a poor candidate in a state of d who has been well and worthily recommended, regularly proposed and approved in open Lodge, and now comes, of his own free will and accord, properly prepared, humbly soliciting to be admitted to the mysteries and privileges of Freemasonry.

IG — How does he hope to obtain those privileges?

Tyler *prompting Can aloud* — By the help of God, being free and of good report *(Can repeats)*.

IG — Halt, while I report to the WM — *closes and locks door, returns to position in front of his chair, Sp EA Sn which he holds.*

IG — WM, — *names Can* — Mr ......, a poor candidate in a state of d who has been well and worthily recommended, regularly proposed and approved in open Lodge and now comes, of his own free will and accord, properly prepared, humbly soliciting to be admitted to the mysteries and privileges of Freemasonry.

WM — How does he hope to obtain those privileges?

IG — By the help of God, being free and of good report.

WM — The tongue of good report has already been heard in his favour. Do you, Brother IG, vouch that he is properly prepared?

IG — I do, WM.

WM — Then let him be admitted in due form.

IG *cuts Sn.*

WM — Brother Deacons.

SD *places kneeling stool in position.*

IG *takes p and goes to door followed by* **JD** *and* **SD,** *JD on left.*

IG *opens door, retaining hold on it as before, presents p to Can's n l b.*

IG Do you feel anything? — *and after an affirmative answer from Can raises the p above his head to show that he has so presented it.*

JD *with l h takes Can firmly by r h (***S D** *on Can's left) and leads him to the kneeling*

C

stool. All three stand facing E.

IG *after Can is admitted, closes and locks door, places p on SW's pedestal and resumes his seat.*

WM *names Can* — Mr ......, as no person can be made a Mason unless he is free and of mature age, I demand of you, are you a free man and of the full age of twenty-one years?

JD *prompting Can aloud* — I am *(Can repeats).*

WM — Thus assured, I will thank you to kneel while the blessing of Heaven is invoked on our proceedings.

 JD *assists Can to kneel, instructing him if necessary in a whisper, and then releases his r h.*

WM *one* ⊣ **SW** *one* ⊣ **JW** *one* ⊣

Ds *hold wands in l h, cross them over head of Can and give Sn of R.*

ALL *stand with Sn of R (Can does not give Sn of R).*

PRAYER

(***WM** *says prayer in E L of I.*)

Vouchsafe Thine aid, Almighty Father and Supreme Governor of the Universe, to our present convention, and grant that this Candidate for Freemasonry may so dedicate and devote his life to Thy service as to become a true and faithful brother among us. Endue him with a competency of Thy divine wisdom, that, assisted by the secrets of our Masonic art, he may the better be enabled to unfold the beauties of true godliness, to the honour and glory of Thy Holy Name.

*IPM — So mote it be.

ALL *drop Sn of R.*

Ds *uncross wands and hold them again in r hs.*

WM — In all cases of difficulty and danger, in whom do you put your trust?

JD *prompting Can aloud* — In ...... (*Can repeats*).

WM — Right glad am I to find your faith so well founded: relying on such sure

*See Notes on Ritual and Procedure.

support you may safely rise and follow your leader with a firm but humble confidence, for where the name of . . . . . . is invoked, we trust no danger can ensue.

WM *sits.*

JD *assists Can to rise, taking his r h firmly as before.*

ALL (*except* **Ds** *and Can.*) *sit.*

SD *draws kneeling stool aside to his left out of way of JD and Can.*

WM *one* ➞ **SW** *one* ➞ **JW** *one* ➞

WM — The Brethren from the N, E, S and W will take notice that Mr . . . . . . is about to pass in view before them to show that he is the Candidate, properly prepared, and a fit and proper person to be made a Mason.

JD *keeping hold of Can's r h firmly as before instructs him in a whisper to step off with the l f, and begins the perambulation by leading him up the N to N E corner of Lodge, which is 'squared', then past WM to S E corner where the Lodge is again 'squared', and finally to E of JW's pedestal where they stand parallel to the pedestal,* *and a convenient distance from it. JD instructs Can at each corner, after 'squaring,' to step off with l f. These instructions are whispered.*

SD *meanwhile replaces kneeling stool in normal position and when JD and Can have passed N E corner, takes p from SW's pedestal to W M and resumes seat.*

JD *holding Can's r h firmly, strikes JW on r shoulder thrice with Can's r h.*

JW — Whom have you there?

JD — Mr . . . . . . , a poor Candidate in a state of d who has been well and worthily recommended, regularly proposed and approved in open Lodge, and now comes, of his own free will and accord, properly prepared, humbly soliciting to be admitted to the mysteries and privileges of Freemasonry.

JW — How does he hope to obtain those privileges?

JD — By the help of God, being free and of good report.

JW *rises and faces Can.*

JD *places r h of Can in that of JW.*

JW — Enter, free and of good report —

replaces r h of Can in l h of JD and sits.

JD *holding Can's r h firmly leads him to S W corner of the Lodge, which is 'squared', and then to S of SW's pedestal where they stand parallel to the pedestal, and a convenient distance from it.*

JD *holding Can's r h firmly, strikes SW on r shoulder thrice with Can's r h.*

SW — Whom have you there?

JD — Mr . . . . . . , a poor Candidate in a state of d who has been well and worthily recommended, regularly proposed and approved in open Lodge, and now comes, of his own free will and accord, properly prepared, humbly soliciting to be admitted to the mysteries and privileges of Free-masonry.

SW — How does he hope to obtain those privileges?

JD — By the help of God, being free and of good report.

SW *rises and faces Can.*

JD *places r h of Can in that of SW.*

SW — Enter, free and of good report — *replaces Can's r h in l h of JD and remains standing.*

JD *holding Can's r h firmly leads him to N of SW's pedestal, makes an anti-clockwise wheel, places Can's r h in l h of SW and turns Can to face E: he stands on l of Can also facing E.*

SW *holding up Can's r h, Sp and EA Sn* — WM, I present to you Mr . . . . . . , a Can properly prepared to be made a Mason — *maintains Sn and continues to hold Can's r h.*

WM — Bro SW, your presentation shall be attended to, for which purpose I shall address a few questions to the Can which I trust he will answer with candour.

SW *cuts Sn, replaces Can's r h in l h of JD and sits.*

JD *takes Cn's r h from SW and positions himself on r of Can still holding Can's h, both facing E.*

WM *to Can* — Do you seriously declare on your honour that, unbiassed by the improper solicitation of friends against your own inclination, and uninfluenced by mercenary or other unworthy motive, you freely and voluntarily offer yourself a Can for the mysteries and privileges of Freemasonry?

JD *prompting Can aloud* — I do (*Can repeats*).

WM — Do you likewise pledge yourself that you are prompted to solicit those privileges by a favourable opinion pre-conceived of the Institution, a general desire of knowledge, and a sincere wish to render yourself more extensively serviceable to your fellow-creatures?

JD *prompting Can aloud* — I do (*Can repeats*).

WM — Do you further seriously declare on your honour that, avoiding fear on the one hand and rashness on the other, you will steadily persevere through the cer-emony of your Initiation, and if once ad-mitted, you will afterwards act and abide by the ancient usages and established customs of the Order?

JD *prompting Can aloud* — I do (*Can repeats*).

WM — Bro SW, you will direct the JD to instruct the Can to advance to the pedestal in due form.

SW — Bro JD, it is the WM's command that you instruct the Can to advance to the pedestal in due form.

JD *instructs Can to step off with l f and leads him diagonally to position facing WM and about four feet from the pedestal, and, still holding Can's hand, instructs him in a whisper to place his f...t together, then to turn out his r f so as to form a square (ie, the l f pointing E and the r f pointing S).*

JD *aloud to Can and ensuring Can suits action to word* — Take a s p with your l f, bringing the hs together in the form of a square. Take another, a little longer, h to h as before. Another, still longer, hs together as before. (*Can should arrive so that he can kneel without further advancing, and with his l f directed to the E and his r f in the form of a square directed S*).

SD *takes up position on l of Can simultaneously with arrival of latter and JD so that all three stand facing WM, JD on r and SD on l of Can.*

WM — It is my duty to inform you that Masonry is free, and requires a perfect freedom of inclination in every Can for its mysteries. It is founded on the purest principles of piety and virtue. It possesses

great and invaluable privileges, and in order
to secure those privileges to worthy men,
and we trust to worthy men alone, vows of
fidelity are required; but let me assure you
that in those vows there is nothing
incompatible with your civil, moral, or
religious duties. Are you therefore willing to
take a S O, founded on the principles I have
stated, to keep inviolate the secrets and
mysteries of the Order?

Candidate — I am. (*If Can does not
answer voluntarily,* **JD** *should whisper to
him 'Answer'. The Can is supposed to give
this answer of his own free will and he is at
liberty to refuse. If he does so, the ceremony
cannot continue and he is led out of the
Lodge.*)

WM — Then you will kneel on your l k,
your r f formed in a square (*Can does so*);
give me your r h which I place on the VSL
— *does so* — while your l will be employed
in supporting these Cs, one pt presented to
your n l b.*

JD *assists by raising Can's r h on
reference to r h.*

*See Notes on Ritual and Procedure.

SD *assists by raising Can's l h on reference to l h.*

WM *places one leg of Cs in Can's l h and directs the pt to his n l b. The Cs are held by Can with upper pt on b.*

*WM one ➤— **SW** one ➤— **JW** one ➤—

ALL *stand with Sp and EA Sn.*

Ds *hold wands in l h, cross them over head of Can, Sp and EA Sn.*

WM *to Can* — Repeat your name at length and say after me:—

I, ... — *Can gives name in full* — in the presence of the Great Architect of the Universe, and of this worthy, worshipful, and warranted Lodge of Free and Accepted Masons , regularly assembled and properly dedicated, of my own free will and accord, do hereby — *with l h touches Can's r h* — and hereon — *with l h touches VSL* — sincerely and solemnly promise and swear, that I will always h* (*pronounced hail*) conceal, and never reveal any part or parts, point or points of the secrets or mysteries of or belonging to Free and Accepted

**See Notes on Ritual and Procedure.*

Masons in Masonry which may heretofore have been known by me, or shall now or at any future period be communicated to me, unless it be to a true and lawful Brother or Brothers, and not even to him or them, until after due trial, strict examination, or sure information from a well-known Brother that he or they are worthy of that confidence; or in the body of a just, perfect and regular Lodge of Ancient Freemasons. I further solemnly promise that I will not write those secrets, indite, carve, mark, engrave, or otherwise them delineate, or cause or suffer it to be so done by others, if in my power to prevent it, on anything, movable or immovable, under the canopy of Heaven, whereby or whereon any letter, character, or figure, or the least trace of a letter, character, or figure, may become legible, or intelligible to myself or anyone in the world, so that our secret arts and hidden mysteries may improperly become known through my unworthiness. These several points I solemnly swear to observe, without evasion, equivocation, or mental reservation of any kind,

(For Lodges using traditional form of Obl)

> under no less a penalty, on the violation
> of any of them than that of having my t c
> a, my t t o b t r *(singular)* and b i t s
> *(singular)* o t s at l w m, or a cs l f t s,
> where t t r e a f t i 24 hs,

(For Lodges using permissive alternative form of Obl)

> ever bearing in mind the traditional
> penalty on the violation of any of them,
> that of having the t c a , the t t o b t r
> *(singular)* and b i t s *(singular)* o t s at l w
> m, or a cs l f t s, where t t r e a f t i 24 hs,

(Continue for either form)

or the more effective punishment of being
branded as a wilfully perjured individual,
void of all moral worth, and totally unfit to
be received into this worshipful Lodge, or
any other warranted Lodge, or society of
men who prize honour and virtue above the
external advantages of rank and fortune. So
help me God, and keep me steadfast in this
my G and S O of an EA FM.

ALL *cut Sn.*

*See Notes on Ritual and Procedure.

Ds *lower wands to r h.*

WM *removes Cs from Can's l h.*

SD *lowers Can's l h to side. Can's r h remains on VSL.*

WM — What you have repeated may be considered but a serious promise; as a pledge of your fidelity, and to render it a S O, you will seal it with your lips on the VSL* (Can does so).

JD *if necessary instructs Can in whisper.*

WM — Having been kept for a considerable time in a state of d, what, in your present situation, is the predominant wish of your heart?

JD *prompting Can aloud* — L *(Can repeats).*

WM — Bro JD, let that blessing be restored to the Can.

JD *should catch WM's eye to indicate that he is ready.*

WM *raises gavel, moves it l, r, and down.*

ALL *give one clap as gavel strikes pedestal.*

JD *removes h w at the same moment.*

WM *pausing till Can is used to l and ready to continue* — Having been restored to the blessing of material l, let me point out to your attention what we consider the three great, though emblematical, ls in Freemasonry: they are the VSL, the Sq, and Cs. The Sacred Writings are to govern our faith, the Sq to regulate our actions, and the Cs to keep us in due bounds with all mankind, particularly our Brethren in Freemasonry.

WM *takes Can's r h from VSL with his r h* — Rise, newly obligated Brother among Masons — *restores Can's r h to JD.*

WM *sits.*

SD *returns to seat.*

ALL (*except* **JD** *and Can*) *sit.*

JD *takes Can's r h turns l and conducts him to N side of WM's pedestal so that both are in a position parallel to the pedestal and about two feet from it, facing S towards WM, and releases h.*

WM *to Can* — You are now enabled to discover the three lesser ls; they are situated E, S, and W, and are meant to represent the Sn, Mn, and M of the Lodge; the Sn to rule the day, the Mn to govern the night, and the M to rule and direct his Lodge.

(Traditional form)

WM — Bro ....., by your meek and candid behaviour this evening you have escaped two great dangers, but there is a third which will await you until the latest period of your existence.

(Permissive alternative form)

WM — Bro ....., by your meek and candid behaviour this evening you have escaped two great dangers, but traditionally there was a third which would have awaited you until the latest period of your existence.

(Continue for either form)

WM — The dangers you have escaped are those of s and s, for on your entrance into the Lodge this p — *picks up p from pedestal, unsheathes it, and shows it to Can* — was presented to your n l b, so that had you rashly attempted to rush forward, you would have been accessary to your own ...... by ......, whilst the Brother who held it would have remained firm and done his duty — *sheathes p and replaces it on pedestal.*

JD *removes c t from n of Can and hands*

FIRST DEGREE

it to WM.

WM *shows c t to Can* — There was likewise this c t, with a running noose about your n, which would have rendered any attempt at retreat equally fatal — *hands c t to IPM.*

(*Traditional form*)

WM — But the danger which will await you until your latest hour is the penalty of your Obl, of having y t c a, should you improperly disclose the secrets of Masonry.

(*Permissive alternative form*)

WM — But the danger which would, traditionally, have awaited you until your latest hour was the penalty referred to in your Obl, of having the t c a should you improperly disclose the secrets of Masonry.

(*Continue for either form*)

WM — Having taken the G and S O of a Mason, I am now permitted to inform you that there are several degrees in Freemasonry, and peculiar secrets restricted to each; these, however, are not communicated indiscriminately, but are conferred on Candidates according to merit and abilities. I shall therefore proceed to entrust you with the secrets of this Degree, or those marks by which we are known to each other and distinguished from the rest of the world; but must premise for your general information that all Sqs, Ls, and Pdrs are true and proper Sns to know a Mason by. You are therefore expected to stand perfectly erect (*Can does so*), your feet formed in a Sq (*Can does so*), your body being thus considered an emblem of your mind, and your feet of the rectitude of your actions.

WM — You will now take a short pace towards me with your l f, bringing the r h into its h (*Can does so*). That is the f r s in Freemasonry, and it is in this position that the secrets of the Degree are communicated. They consist of a Sn, Tn and Wd — *rises, faces Can and takes Sp.* Place your h i t p w t t e i t f o a s t t l o t w — *illustrates and ensures that Can copies* — The Sn is given b d t h s a t t a d i t t s — *illustrates and ensures Can copies.*
(*Traditional form*)

WM — This is in allusion to the penalty of your Obl implying that as a man of honour and a Mason you would rather have y t c a — *gives P Sn and ensures that Can copies* — than improperly disclose the secrets entrusted to you.

(*Permissive alternative form*)

WM — This is in allusion to the traditional penalty referred to in your Obl, implying that as a man of honour, a Mason would rather have his t c a — *gives P Sn and ensures that Can copies* — than improperly disclose the secrets entrusted to him.

(*Continue for either form*)

WM — The G or Tn is given — *takes Can's r h and adjusts g by placing Can's t in position before placing his own* — by a d p o t t o t f j o t h. This, when regularly given and received serves to distinguish a Brother by n as well as by d. This G or Tn demands a word, a word highly prized amongst Masons as a guard to their privileges. Too much caution, therefore, cannot be observed in communicating it; it should never be given at length, but always by Ls or Ss, to enable you to do which, I must first tell you what that word is: it is ......

JD *repeats word aloud and ensures that Can repeats it aloud after him.*

WM *spells the word.*

JD *spells word aloud and ensures that Can spells it aloud after him.*

WM *retains g* — As in the course of the ceremony you will be called on for this word, the JD will now dictate the answers you are to give. What is this?

JD *prompting Can aloud* — The G or Tn of an EA FM (*Can repeats*).

WM — What does it demand?

JD *prompting Can aloud* — A word (*Can repeats*).

WM — Give me that word.

JD *prompting Can aloud (if necessary by phrases) and quickly to prevent him giving word at length* — At my initiation I was taught to be cautious; I will letter or halve it with you (*Can repeats*).

WM — Which you please, and begin.

(*At this stage the word is halved.*)

JD *gives first half (Can repeats).*

WM *gives second half.*

JD *gives complete word (Can repeats).*

WM — This word is derived from the l h p at the p...way or e...e of K S T, so named after ......, the G G of D, a P and R in I. The import of the word is — In ......; pass, ... — *places Can's r h in l h of* **JD** *and sits.*

JD *turns right, controlling Can by holding his r h, regains floor of Lodge, turns l, instructs Can in whisper to step off with l f, passes in front of WM's ped to the S E corner which they 'square'. JD leads Can to E side of JW's pedestal, where they stand parallel to the pedestal and a convenient distance from it. Releases h.**

JD *rests butt of his wand on floor, with top resting against r shoulder, Sp and EA Sn* — Bro JW, I present to you Bro ...... on his initiation — *Cuts Sn and takes wand in r h again.*

JW — I will thank Bro ...... to advance to me as a Mason.

JD *instructs Can in a whisper to take Sp and give EA Sn and then to cut Sn, and*

**See Notes on Ritual and Procedure.*

ensures Can does so.

JW –– Have you anything to communicate?

JD *prompting Can aloud* — I have (*Can repeats*).

JW *rises, faces Can, and takes Sp and offers hand.*

JD *places r h of Can in that of JW, and with l h adjusts g from above.*

JW *gives g, after JD has adjusted Can's r t, retaining g throughout the whole of colloquy* — What is this?

JD *prompting Can aloud* — The G or Tn of an EA FM (*Can repeats*).

JW — What does it demand?

JD *prompting Can aloud* — A word (*Can repeats*).

JW — Give me that word.

JD *prompting Can aloud (quickly and, if necessary, by phrases)* — At my initiation I was taught to be cautious; I will letter or halve it with you (*Can repeats in similar phrases*).

JW Which you please and begin.
(*At the JW's ped the word is first lettered then halved*)

JD *gives first letter aloud (Can repeats).*

JW *gives second letter.*

JD *gives third letter (Can repeats).*

JW *gives fourth letter.*

JD *gives first half (Can repeats).*

JW *gives second half.*

JD *gives whole word (Can repeats).*

JW — Pass, ... — *replaces Can's r h in l h of JD and sits.*

JD *leads Can via SW corner of the Lodge, 'squaring' as before, to the S of SW's pedestal. Both Can and JD face N parallel to SW's pedestal and a convenient distance from it. Releases h.*

JW *rests butt of wand on floor with the top resting against r shoulder, Sp and EA Sn — Bro SW, I present to you Bro ...... on his initiation — cuts Sn and takes wand in his r h again.*

SW — I will thank Bro ...... to advance to me as a Mason.

JD *instructs Can in whisper to take Sp only and ensures he does not give Sn at this stage.*

SW — What is that?

See Notes on Ritual and Procedure.

JD *prompting Can aloud* — The f r sp in Freemasonry (*Can repeats*).

SW — Do you bring anything else?

JD *prompting Can aloud* — I do (*Can repeats*).

JD *instructs Can to give EA Sn and cut it.*

SW — What is that?

JD *prompting Can aloud* — The Sn of an EA FM (*Can repeats*).

SW — To what does it allude?

JD *prompting Can aloud and by suitable phrases* (*Can repeating*).

(*Traditional form*)

The penalty of my Obl, implying that as a man of honour and a Mason I would rather have my t c a — *as Can says 'my t c a' prompts him to give Sn and cut it* — than improperly disclose the secrets entrusted to me.

(*Permissive alternative form*)

The traditional penalty referred to in my Obl, implying that, as a man of honour, a Mason would rather have his t c a — *as Can says 'his t c a', prompts him to give Sn and cut it* — than improperly

‖ disclose the secrets entrusted to him.

(Continue for either form)

SW — Have you anything to communicate?

JD *prompting Can aloud* — I have *(Can repeats)*.

SW *rises, faces Can, takes Sp and offers hand.*

JD *places Can's r h in that of SW and with l h adjusts g from above.*

SW *gives g after JD has adjusted Can's r t and retains g throughout the whole of the colloquy* — What is this?

JD *prompting Can aloud* — The G or T of an EA FM *(Can repeats)*.

SW — What does it demand?

JD *prompting Can aloud* — A word *(Can repeats)*.

SW — Give me that word.

JD *prompting Can aloud (quickly and if necessary by phrases)* — At my initiation I was taught to be cautious; I will letter or halve it with you *(Can repeats in phrases)*.

SW — Which you please, and begin.

(Here the word is halved).

JD *gives first half aloud (Can repeats)*.

SW *gives second half.*

JD *gives whole word (Can repeats).*

SW — Whence is this word derived?

JD *prompting Can aloud by phrases* —
From the l h p at the p...way or e...e of K S
T, so named after ..., the G G of D, a P and
R in I (*Can repeats in phrases*).

SW — The import of the word?

JD *prompting Can aloud* — In .... (*Can
repeats*).

SW — Pass, ... — *replaces Can's r h
in l h of JD and remains standing.*

JD *takes Can by r h to N side of SW's
pedestal, by passing in front of it. He then
makes an anti-clockwise wheel, places
Can's r h in l h of SW and lining up on l of
Can ensures they are both facing E.*

SW *Sp and EA Sn which he holds* —
WM, I present to you Bro ...... on his
initiation for some mark of your favour.

WM — Bro SW, I delegate you to invest
him with the distinguishing badge of a
Mason.

SW *cuts Sn, releases Can's h and with
Can facing him, puts on him badge of an
EA FM.*

JD *assists if necessary.*

SW *picks up lower r h corner of badge with his l h, to Can* — Bro ...... by the WM's command, I invest you with the distinguishing badge of a Mason. It is more ancient than the Golden Fleece or Roman Eagle, more honourable than the Garter or any other Order in existence, being the badge of innocence and the bond of friendship. I strongly exhort you ever to wear and consider it as such; and further inform you that if you never disgrace that badge — *strikes badge of Can with his r h* (**ALL** *Brethren strike theirs simultaneously*) — it will never disgrace you — *with his l h restores r h of Can to l h of JD and sits.*

JD *takes Can's r h from SW and positions himself on r of Can, both facing E, and releases h.*

WM — Let me add to the observations of the SW, that you are never to put on that badge should you be about to visit a Lodge in which there is a Brother with whom you are at variance, or against whom you entertain animosity. In such cases it is expected that you will invite him to withdraw in order amicably to settle your differences, which being happily effected, you may then clothe yourselves, enter the Lodge and work with that love and harmony which should at all times characterise Freemasons. But if, unfortunately, your differences be of such a nature as not to be so easily adjusted, it were better that one or both of you retire than that the harmony of the Lodge should be disturbed by your presence.

WM — Bro JD, you will place our new-made Brother at the N E part of the Lodge.

JD *takes Can's r h leads him up N to N E part of Lodge. Both face S, as near as convenient to the corner of the Lodge. JD releases h.*

JD *to Can* — L f across the Lodge, r f down the Lodge; pay attention to the WM — *ensures Can forms square with his ft.*

WM — It is customary, at the erection of all stately and superb edifices, to lay the first or foundation stone at the N E corner of the building. You, being newly admitted into Masonry, are placed at the N E part of

the Lodge figuratively to represent that
stone, and from the foundation laid this
evening may you raise a superstructure
perfect in its parts and honourable to the
builder. You now stand, to all external
appearance, a just and upright Mason and
I give it you in strong terms of recommendation ever to continue and act as such.
Indeed, I shall immediately proceed to put
your principles in some measure to the test,
by calling upon you to exercise that virtue
which may justly be denominated the
distinguishing characteristic of a
Freemason's heart — I mean Charity. I
need not here dilate on its excellences; no
doubt it has often been felt and practised by
you. Suffice it to say, it has the approbation
of Heaven and earth, and like its sister,
Mercy, blesses him who gives as well as
him who receives.

In a society so widely extended as
Freemasonry, the branches of which are
spread over the four quarters of the globe, it
cannot be denied that we have many
members of rank and opulence; neither can
it be concealed that among the thousands

who range under its banners, there are
some who, perhaps from circumstances of
unavoidable calamity and misfortune, are
reduced to the lowest ebb of poverty and
distress. On their behalf it is our usual
custom to awaken the feelings of every
new-made Brother by such a claim on his
charity as his circumstances in life may
fairly warrant. Whatever, therefore, you
feel disposed to give, you will deposit with
the JD; it will be thankfully received and
faithfully applied.

JD *moves to a position in front of WM
and facing Can, holds out l h (or alms-dish
if he has been handed one) and makes
appeal* —

JD — Have you anything to give in the
cause of Charity?

Candidate — ......

JD *lowers hand or alms-dish and, if Can
does not answer quickly, proceeds with
second question* — Were you deprived of
everything v...l...e previously to entering the
Lodge?

Candidate *gives affirmative.*

JD — If you had not been so deprived

would you give freely?

Candidate *gives affirmative.*

JD *turns r and faces WM, Sp and EA Sn which he holds, and retains wand in crook of r shoulder* — WM, our new-made Brother affirms that he was deprived of everything v...l...e previously to entering the Lodge or he would give freely — *cuts Sn and resumes position on r of Can.*

WM — I congratulate you on the honourable sentiments by which you are actuated; likewise on the inability which in the present instance precludes you from gratifying them. Believe me, this trial was not made with a view to sport with your feelings; far be from us any such intention. It was done for three especial reasons: first, as I have already premised, to put your principles to the test; secondly, to evince to the Brethren that you had neither m...y nor m...c substance about you, for if you had, the ceremony of your initiation thus far, must have been repeated; and thirdly, as a warning to your own heart, that should you at any future period meet a Brother in distressed circumstances who might solicit your assistance, you will remember the peculiar moment you were received into Masonry, poor and penniless, and cheerfully embrace the opportunity of practising that virtue you have professed to admire.

IPM *places w ts in readiness on WM's pedestal if he has not previously done so.*

JD *takes Can's r h and places him in front of WM, in a position as close as convenient to pedestal and releases h.*

WM — I now present to you the w ts of an EA FM: they are the 24-in G, the common G, and C, — *indicates ts as he names them* — The 24-in G is to measure our work, the common G to knock off all superfluous knobs and excrescences, and the C to further smooth and prepare the stone and render it fit for the hands of the more expert workman. But, as we are not all operative Masons, but rather free and accepted or speculative, we apply these ts. to our morals. In this sense, the 24-in G represents the twenty-four hours of the day, part to be spent in prayer to Almighty God, part in labour and refreshment, and part in serving a friend or Brother in time of need, without detriment to ourselves or connections. The common G represents the force of conscience, which should keep down all vain and unbecoming thoughts which might obtrude during any of the aforementioned periods, so that our words and actions may ascend unpolluted to the Throne of Grace. The C points out to us the advantages of education, by which means alone we are rendered fit members of regularly organised Society.

WM — As in the course of the evening you will be called on for certain fees for your initiation, it is proper you should know by what authority we act. This is our Charter or Warrant from the Grand Lodge of England — *opens and shows Warrant of Lodge to Can* — which is for your inspection on this or any future evening. This is the Book of Constitutions — *hands Can a copy* — and these are our By-laws — *hands Can a copy* — both of which I recommend to your serious perusal, as by one you will be instructed in the duties you owe to the Craft in general, and by the other in those you owe to this Lodge in particular.

WM — You are now at liberty to retire in order to restore yourself to your personal comforts, and on your return to the Lodge, I shall call your attention to a Charge, founded on the excellences of the Institution and the qualifications of its members.

JD *takes Can by r h and guiding him moves anti-clockwise so as to face W and takes Can directly, no 'squaring', to N of SW's pedestal. Here he wheels Can clockwise so as to face E, halts and releases h.*

JD *to Can aloud* — Salute the WM as a Mason — *instructs Can in whisper to take Sp and give EA Sn and cut it, and ensures Can does so.*

JD *takes Can by r h, makes an anti-clockwise wheel and conducts him to the door.*

IG *goes to door in front of JD and opens it, closing and locking it again after Can has gone out.*

JD *and* **IG** *resume seats.*

Outside Lodge Can resumes his ordinary

dress with EA badge. When Can is ready,
Tyler *gives EA ks on door of Lodge.*

IG *rises in front of his chair, Sp and EA
Sn* — Bro JW, there is a report — *holds
Sn.*

JW *seated, one* ▬▬◗

IG *cuts Sn, goes to door, opens it, and
looks out without speaking.*

Tyler — The Can on his return.

IG *makes no reply, closes and locks
door, returns to position in front of his
chair, Sp and EA Sn which he holds* —
WM, the Can on his return.

WM — Admit him.

IG *cuts Sn, awaits arrival of JD and
goes to door.*

JD *follows IG to door.*

IG *opens door and admits Can.*

JD *receives Can and conducts him by r h
to N of SW's pedestal both facing E.
Releases h.* *

IG *when JD has received Can, closes
and locks door, returns to chair and sits.*

JD *to Can* — Salute the WM as a
Mason — *instructs Can if necessary and*

*See Notes on Ritual and Procedure.

*ensures he takes Sp and gives EA Sn and
cuts it. Both remain standing without
handclasp at N of SW's pedestal while the
Charge is delivered.*

CHARGE AFTER INITIATION

*(**WM** delivers this Charge in E L of Imp)

Bro ......, as you have passed through the
ceremony of your initiation, let me
congratulate you on being admitted a
member of our ancient and honourable
institution. Ancient no doubt it is, as having
subsisted from time immemorial, and
honourable it must be acknowledged to be,
as by a natural tendency it conduces to
make those so who are obedient to its
precepts. Indeed, no institution can boast a
more solid foundation than that on which
Freemasonry rests — the practice of every
moral and social virtue. And to so high an
eminence has its credit been advanced that
in every age monarchs themselves have
been promoters of the art, have not thought
it derogatory to their dignity to exchange
the sceptre for the trowel, have patronised

See Notes on Ritual and Procedure.

our mysteries and joined in our assemblies.

As a Freemason, let me recommend to your most serious contemplation the V S L, charging you to consider it as the unerring standard of truth and justice and to regulate your actions by the divine precepts it contains. Therein you will be taught the important duties you owe to God, to your neighbour and to yourself. To God, by never mentioning His name but with that awe and reverence which are due from the creature of his Creator, by imploring His aid in all your lawful undertakings, and by looking up to Him in every emergency for comfort and support. To your neighbour, by acting with him on the square, by rendering him every kind office which justice or mercy may require, by relieving his necessities and soothing his afflictions, and by doing to him as in similar cases you would wish he would do to you. And to yourself, by such a prudent and well-regulated course of discipline as may best conduce to the preservation of your corporeal and mental faculties in their fullest energy, thereby enabling you to exert those talents wherewith God has blessed you, as well to His glory as the welfare of your fellow creatures.

As a citizen of the world, I am to enjoin you to be exemplary in the discharge of your civil duties, by never proposing or at all countenancing any act that may have a tendency to subvert the peace and good order of society, by paying due obedience to the laws of of any State which may for a time become the place of your residence or afford you its protection, and above all, by never losing sight of the allegiance due to the Sovereign of your native land, ever remembering that nature has implanted in your breast a sacred and indissoluble attachment towards that country whence you derived your birth and infant nurture.

As an individual, let me recommend the practice of every domestic as well as public virtue: let Prudence direct you, Temperance chasten you, Fortitude support you, and Justice be the guide of all your actions. Be especially careful to maintain in their fullest splendour those truly Masonic ornaments, which have already been amply illustrated

— Benevolence and Charity.

Still, as a Freemason, there are other excellences of character to which your attention may be peculiarly and forcibly directed: amongst the foremost of these are Secrecy, Fidelity and Obedience. Secrecy consists in an inviolable adherence to the Obligation you have entered into — never improperly to disclose any of those Masonic secrets which have now been, or may at any future period be, entrusted to your keeping, and cautiously to avoid all occasions which may inadvertently lead you so to do. Your Fidelity must be exemplified by a strict observance of the Constitutions of the fraternity, by adhering to the ancient landmarks of the Order, by never attempting to extort or otherwise unduly obtain the secrets of a superior degree, and by refraining from recommending anyone to a participation of our secrets unless you have strong grounds to believe that by a similar fidelity he will ultimately reflect honour on your choice. Your Obedience must be proved by a strict observance of our laws and regulations, by prompt attention to all signs and summonses, by modest and correct demeanour in the Lodge, by abstaining from every topic of political or religious discussion, by a ready acquiescence in all votes and resolutions duly passed by a majority of the brethren, and by perfect submission to the Master and his Wardens whilst acting in the discharge of their respective offices.

And as a last general recommendation, let me exhort you to dedicate yourself to such pursuits as may at once enable you to be respectable in life, useful to mankind, and an ornament to the society of which you have this day become a member; to study more especially such of the liberal Arts and Sciences as may lie within the compass of your attainment, and without neglecting the ordinary duties of your station, to endeavour to make a daily advancement in Masonic knowledge.

From the very commendable attention you appear to have given to this charge, I am led to hope you will duly appreciate the value of Freemasonry, and indelibly imprint on your heart the sacred dictates of Truth, of Honour, and of Virtue.

JD *leads Can to seat beside SD and resumes his seat.*

SECOND DEGREE
OR
CEREMONY OF PASSING

QUESTIONS BEFORE PASSING

The Lodge is open in the First Degree.

WM *requests EAs other than Can to withdraw and indicates with appropriate words that the next business is to pass Bro ......*

JD *goes to Can, takes him by r h and leads him to position N of SW's ped both facing E and releases h.*

WM — Brethren, Bro ...... is this evening a Can to be passed to the Second Degree, but it is first requisite that he give proofs of proficiency in the former. I shall therefore proceed to put the necessary questions — *to Can* — Where were you first prepared to be made a Mason?

JD *must be prepared, if necessary, to prompt Can.*

Can — In my h.

WM — Where next?

Can — In a convenient room adjoining the Lodge.

WM — Describe the mode of your preparation.

Can — I was d...v...d of m...l and h...w...d. My r a, l b, and k were made b, my r h was s s and a c t placed about my n.

WM — Where were you made a Mason?

Can — In the body of a Lodge, just, perfect, and regular.

WM — And when?

Can — When the sun was at its meridian.

WM — In this country Freemasons' Lodges are usually held in the evening; how do you account for that which at first view appears a paradox?

Can — The earth constantly revolving on its axis in its orbit round the sun and Freemasonry being universally spread over its surface, it necessarily follows that the sun must always be at its meridian with respect to Freemasonry.

WM — What is Freemasonry?

Can — A peculiar system of morality,

veiled in allegory and illustrated by symbols.

WM — Name the grand principles on which the Order is founded.

Can — Brotherly love, relief and truth.

WM — Who are fit and proper persons to be made Masons?

Can — Just, upright and free men, of mature age, sound judgment, and strict morals.

WM — How do you know yourself to be a Mason?

Can — By the regularity of my initiation, repeated trials and approbations, and a willingness at all times to undergo an examination when properly called on.

WM — How do you demonstrate the p of your being a Mason to others?

Can — By sns, ts, and the perfect pts of my entrance.

WM — These are the usual questions: I will put others if any Brother wishes me to do so.

JD conducts Can by r h direct to N side of WM's ped and a convenient distance from it, both facing S. Releases hand.

WM — Do you pledge your honour as a man, and your fidelity as a Mason, that you will steadily persevere through the ceremony of being passed to the Degree of a FC?

JD *prompting Can aloud* — I do *(Can repeats).*

(For Lodges using traditional form of Obl.)

WM — Do you likewise pledge yourself under the penalty of your Obl that you will conceal what I shall now impart to you with the same strict caution as the other secrets in Masonry?

(For Lodges using permissive alternative form of Obl.)

WM — Do you likewise pledge yourself that you will conceal what I shall now impart to you with the same strict caution as the other secrets in Masonry?

(Continue for either form.)

JD *prompting Can aloud* — I do *(Can repeats).*

WM — Then I will entrust you with a test of merit, which is a p g and p w leading to the Degree to which you seek to be admitted — *rises, faces Can, and takes the latter's r h in his own r h and holds it* — the p g is given — *adjusts p g by placing Can's t in position before placing his own* — by a distinct p of the t between t f a s js o t h. This p g demands a p w, which is ......

JD — *prompting Can, speaks word aloud (Can repeats).*

WM — ...... denotes ...... and is usually depicted in our Lodges by an e o c near to a f o w. You must be particularly careful to remember this word, as without it you cannot gain admission into a Lodge in a superior degree. Pass, ... — *restores Can's r ṅ to l h of JD and sits.*

JD *guiding Can, makes a clockwise wheel and conducts Can direct to N of SW's ped. Here he wheels Can clockwise so as to face E and releases hand.*

JD *to Can aloud* — Salute the WM as a Mason — *instructs Can in whisper to take Sp, give EA Sn and cut it.*

JD *takes Can by r h, makes anti-clockwise wheel with Can and conducts him to door.*

IG *goes to door in front of JD and opens*

it, closing and locking it again when Can has gone out.

IG *and* **JD** *return to seats.*

THE PASSING

WM *conducts Opening the Lodge in Second Degree or Resumes in that degree whichever is appropriate. This will conclude with —*

*WM — FC ▬▬Ɨ *quietly (ie given so as to be audible only in the Lodge).*

*SW — FC ▬▬Ɨ *quietly.* **JW** *— FC* ▬▬Ɨ *quietly.*

*TB is attended to when JW has given ks (usually by JD).

IG *gives ks by r h on l sleeve standing in his place.*

IPM, *meanwhile, exposes one p of Cs.* (No ks are given on door by either IG or Tyler.)*

Tyler *prepares Can including EA badge and Ceremony proceeds:—*

Tyler *gives EA ks on door. This informs Lodge that a Can for Passing is at the door of the Lodge.*

*See Notes on Ritual and Procedure.

IG *rises in front of his chair, Sp and FC Sn* — Bro JW, there is a report — *holds Sn.*

JW *no ks, rises, Sp and FC Sn* — WM, there is a report — *holds Sn.*

WM — Bro JW, inquire who wants admission.

JW *cuts Sn and sits* — Bro IG, see who wants admission.

IG *cuts Sn, goes to door, opens it, checks that Can is properly prepared and remains on threshold with hand on door handle; to Tyler (Colloquy between IG and Tyler should be audible throughout Lodge.)*

IG — Whom have you there?

Tyler *names Can* — Bro ...... who has been regularly initiated into Freemasonry and has made such progress as he hopes will recommend him to be passed to the Degree of a FC, for which ceremony he is properly prepared.

IG — How does he hope to obtain the privileges of the Second Degree?

Tyler — By the help of God, the assistance of the Sq and the benefit of a p w.

IG — Is he in possession of the p w?

Tyler — Will you prove him?

IG *receives p g and p w from Can* (**T** *prompts if necessary.*)

IG — Halt while I report to the WM — *closes and locks door, returns to position in front of his chair, Sp and FC Sn, which he holds.*

IG — WM, — *names Can* — Bro ...... who has been regularly initiated into Freemasonry and has made such progress as he hopes will recommend him to be passed to the Degree of a FC, for which ceremony he is properly prepared.

WM — How does he hope to obtain the privileges of the Second Degree?

IG — By the help of God, the assistance of the Sq and the benefit of a p w.

WM — We acknowledge the propriety of the aid by which he seeks admission. Do you, Bro IG, vouch that he is in possession of the p w?

IG — I do, WM.

WM — Then let him be admitted in due form.

IG *cuts Sn.*

WM — Bro Deacons.

JD *places kneeling stool in position.*

IG *takes Sq and goes to door followed by* **JD** *and* **SD,** *SD on left.*

IG *opens door, retaining hold on it, and applies the angle of the Sq to Can's n l b, and then raises Sq above his head to show that he has so applied it.*

SD *with l h takes Can by r h (* **JD** *on Can's left) and leads him to the kneeling stool about one short pace from it and releases h. All three stand facing E.*

IG *after Can is admitted closes and locks door and resumes his seat.*

SD *to Can* — Advance as a Mason — *and ensures that Can takes Sp, gives and cuts EA Sn.*

WM — Let the Can kneel while the blessing of Heaven is invoked on what we are about to do.

SD *ensures Can kneels and gives Sn of R.*

WM *one* ➼ **SW** *one* ➼ **JW** *one* ➼ .

Ds *hold wands in l h, cross them over head of Can and give Sn of R.*

ALL *stand with Sn of R.*

PRAYER

*(WM *says prayer in E L of I.*)

We supplicate the continuance of Thine aid, O merciful Lord, on behalf of ourselves and him who kneels before Thee. May the work begun in Thy Name be continued to Thy Glory and evermore established in us by obedience to Thy precepts.

*IPM — So mote it be.

ALL *drop Sn of R.*

Ds *uncross wands and hold them again in r h.*

WM — Let the Can rise *(He does so)*

WM *sits.*

ALL *(except* **Ds** *and Can) sit.*

JD *draws kneeling stool aside to his left, out of way of SD and Can.*

SD *takes Can's r h firmly, instructs him in a whisper to step off with the l f and leads Can up N towards E part of Lodge.*

JD *as soon as SD and Can have moved off, replaces kneeling stool in normal position and resumes seat.*

*See Notes on Ritual and Procedure.

SD *leads Can to N E corner where they 'square' the Lodge. SD instructs Can to step off with l f and proceeds with him to point in front of WM's ped, halts there and releases hand.*

SD *to Can* — Salute the WM as a Mason — *ensures Can takes Sp, gives EA Sn and cuts it.*

SD *takes Can's r h, instructs him to step off with l f and conducts him to S E corner where they again 'square' the Lodge. SD again instructs Can to step off with l f and conducts him to E side of JW's ped where they stand parallel to ped and a convenient distance from it. Releases h.*

SD *to Can* — Advance to the JW as such, showing the Sn and communicating the Tn and Wd — *ensures Can takes Sp and gives EA Sn and cuts it.*

JW — Have you anything to communicate?

SD *prompting Can aloud* — I have *(Can repeats).*

JW *rises, faces Can with Sp and offers hand.*

SD *places r h of Can in that of JW and*

adjusts g from above.

JW *gives g after SD has adjusted Can's r t and retains g throughout the whole of the colloquy* — What is this?

SD *prompting Can aloud* — The G or Tn of an EA FM *(Can repeats).*

JW — What does it demand?

SD *prompting Can aloud* — A word *(Can repeats).*

JW — Give me that word freely and at length.

SD *prompting Can aloud* — ...... *(Can repeats).*

JW — Pass, ... — *replaces Can's r h in l h of SD and sits.*

SD *leads Can on to floor of Lodge, instructs him to step off with l f and leads him via S Wt corner which is 'squared' to a point in front of SW's ped, halts and releases hand.*

SD — Salute the SW as a Mason — *ensures Can takes Sp, gives EA Sn and cuts it.*

SD *takes Can's r h, instructs him to step off with l f and leads him to N of SW's ped, wheels clockwise so that both face WM and* *releases hand.*

WM *one* ━┫ **SW** *one* ━┫ **JW** *one* ━┫.

WM — The Brethren will take notice that Bro ......, who has been regularly initiated into Freemasonry, is about to pass in view before them, to show that he is the Can properly prepared to be passed to the Degree of a FC.

SD *takes Can's r h, instructs him to step off with l f and leads him up N side of Lodge, 'squares' NE corner as before, halts in front of WM's ped, and releases h.*

SD — Salute the WM as a Mason — *ensures Can takes Sp, gives EA Sn and cuts it.*

SD *takes Can's r h, instructs him to step off with l f and continues perambulation, 'squaring' S E corner, halts in front of JW's ped and releases h.*

SD — Salute the JW as a Mason — *ensures Can takes Sp gives EA Sn and cuts it.*

SD *takes Can's r h, instructs him to step off with the l f and continues perambulation, 'squaring' S Wt corner, leads Can to*

S of SW's ped where they stand parallel to ped and at a convenient distance from it. Releases h.*

SD — Advance to the SW as such, showing the Sn and communicating the p g and p w you received from the WM previously to leaving the Lodge — *ensures Can takes Sp, gives EA Sn and cuts it.*

SW — Have you anything to communicate?

SD *prompting Can aloud* — I have *(Can repeats).*

SW *rises, faces Can and offers hand.*

SD *places Can's r h in that of SW and with l h adjusts p g from above.*

SW *gives p g after SD has adjusted Can's r t and retains p g throughout colloquy.*

SW — What is this?

SD *prompting Can aloud* — The p g leading from the First to the Second Degree *(Can repeats).*

SW — What does this p g demand?

SD *prompting Can aloud* — A p w *(Can repeats).*

*See Notes on Ritual and Procedure.

SW — Give me that p w.

SD *prompting Can aloud* — ...... *(Can repeats).*

SW — What does ...... denote?

SD *prompting Can aloud* — ...... *(Can repeats).*

SW — How is it usually depicted in our Lodges?

SD *prompting Can aloud* — By an e o c near to a f o w *(Can repeats).*

SW — Pass, ... — *replaces Can's r h in l of SD and remains standing.*

SD *takes Can's r h, leads him on to floor of L, instructs him to step off with l f and conducts him to N side of SW's ped. Here he makes an anti-clockwise wheel and places Can's r h in l of SW: he lines up on l of Can and ensures both are facing E.*

SW *holding up Can's r h, Sp, and Sn of F* — WM, I present to you Bro ......, a Can properly prepared to be passed to the Second Degree — *maintains Sn and continues to hold Can's r h.*

WM — Bro SW, you will direct the SD to instruct the Can to advance to the E in due form.

SW *cuts Sn, replaces Can's r h in l h of SD, and sits.*

SD *takes up a position on r of Can, ensures both face E and releases hand.*

SW — Bro SD, it is the WM's command that you instruct the Can to advance to the E in due form.

SD *takes Can's r h, instructs him to step off with l f and leads Can up N side of Lodge to a convenient distance from N E corner and turns with him so as to face S. Leaving Can, SD moves forward to centre line of Lodge, turns and faces Can.*

SD *to Can* — The method of advancing from W to E in this Degree is by .... as if ascending a w s. For your information I will go through them, and you will afterwards copy me.

SD *then turns about, and stands at a point opposite WM's ped and about three paces from it, facing S. He places his feet at r angles, h to h, r f pointing W and l f pointing S. He steps off with the l f, lifting his ft at each step as if ascending a w s. In doing so he completes a semi-circle starting on the centre line of Lodge and also* *finishing on it in front of WM's ped with r f pointing E, l f pointing N, h to h.*

SD *then returns to Can, following the semi circular line in the reverse direction. He then places Can at the same point opposite WM's ped, releases hand and instructs him to go through prescribed steps by standing in front of him and indicating with wand where Can's ft should fall. He then places himself on Can's r as he completes steps.*

JD *goes to WM's ped and stands on Can's l at same time as Can and SD arrive there. All three are now in front of WM's ped, SD on r and JD on l of Can, all facing E.*

WM — As in every case the Degrees in Freemasonry are to be kept separate and distinct, another Obl will now be required of you, in many respects similar to the former. Are you willing to take it?

Can — I am. *(If Can does not answer voluntarily* **SD** *should whisper to him 'Answer.')*

WM — Then you will kneel on your r k, your l f formed in a sq, *(Can does so)* place your r h on the VSL, *(Can does so)* while your l a will be supported in the angle of the sq.

SD *takes Sq (usually from IPM) and passes it behind Can to JD.*

JD *arranges arm of Can in angle of Sq as in H Sn or Sn of P of Second Degree, arm forwards at r a to bdy, forearm at r a to arm and t projecting backwards in f of a sq. JD supports Sq in his r h.*

WM *one* ▬█ **SW** *one* ▬█ **JW** *one* █.

Ds *hold wands in l h, cross them over head of Can; both take Sp,* **SD** *gives Sn of F.*

ALL *stand, with Sp and Sn of F.*

WM, *to Can* — Repeat your name at length and say after me:

I, ... — *Can gives name in full* — in the presence of the Grand Geometrician of the Universe and of this worthy and worshipful Lodge of FC FMs, regularly held, assembled, and properly dedicated, of my own free will and accord, do hereby — *with l h touches Can's r h* — and hereon — *with l h touches VSL* — solemnly promise and swear that I will always h* *(pronounced hail),* conceal, and never improperly reveal any or either of the ss or mys of or belonging to the Second Degree in Freemasonry, denominated the FC's, to him who is but an EA, any more than I would either of them to the uninstructed and popular world who are not Masons. I further solemnly pledge myself to act as a true and faithful Cn, answer Sns, obey summonses, and maintain the principles inculcated in the former degree. These several points I solemnly swear to observe, without evasion, equivocation, or mental reservation of any kind,

(Traditional form.)

under no less a penalty, on the violation of any of them, than that of having m l b laid o, m h t t, and g t t r bs of the a, or d bts o t f a p.

(Permissive alternative form.)

ever bearing in mind the traditional penalty on the violation of any of them, that of having the l b l o, the h t t, and g t t r bs of the a or d bts. o t f a p.

See Notes on Ritual and Procedure.

(Continue for either form.)

So help me, A G, and keep me steadfast in this my solemn Obl of a FC FM.

ALL *cut Sn.*

Ds *lower wands to r h.*

JD *removes Sq, and passes it behind Can to SD, who replaces it; JD lowers Can's l h to his side.*

WM — As a pledge of your F, and to render this a S O which might otherwise be considered but a serious promise, you will s i w y l t on the VSL *(Can does so — **SD** if necessary instructs in whisper).*

WM — Your progress in Masonry is marked by the position of the S and Cs. When you were made an EA, both pts were hid; in this Degree one is disclosed, implying that you are now in the midway of Freemasonry, superior to an EA, but inferior to that to which I trust you will hereafter attain.

WM *takes Can's r h from VSL with his r h* — Rise, newly obligated FC FM — *restores Can's r h to SD.*

JD *returns to seat.*

WM *sits.*

ALL *sit except* **SD** *and Can.*

SD *takes Can by r h, turns l and leads him to N side of WM's ped so that both are in a position parallel to ped and about two short paces from it facing S towards WM. SD releases hand.*

WM — Having taken the S O of a FC, I shall proceed to entrust you with the secrets of the Degree. You will therefore advance to me as at your initiation.

SD *ensures Can takes Sp and gives EA Sn and cuts it.*

WM — You will now take another short pace towards me with your l f, bringing the r h into its h as before. *(Can does so).* That is the s r s in Freemasonry, and it is in this position that the Scts of the Degree are communicated. They consist, as in the former instance, of a Sn, Tn, and Wd, with this difference, that in this Degree the Sn is of a three-fold nature — *rises, faces Can, with Sp* — The first part of the threefold Sn is called the Sn of F and is given by p t r h on t l b w t t e i t f o a s —*illustrates and ensures Can copies* — emblematically to shield the repository of your secrets from

the attacks of the insidious. The second
part is called the H Sn, or Sn of P, and is
given by t u t l h w t t l e i t f o a s —
illustrates and ensures Can copies — This
took its rise at the time that J fought the
battles of the Lord, when it was in this
position he prayed fervently to the
Almighty to continue the l of d, that he
might complete the overthrow of his
enemies. The third part is the P Sn and is
given by d t l h, d t r s a t b t a d i t t s —
illustrates and ensures Can copies.

(Traditional form.)

   WM — This is in allusion to the P of
your Obl, implying, that as a man of
honour and a FC FM you would rather
have y h t f y bt — *illustrates and
ensures Can copies* — than improperly
disclose the Scts entrusted to you.

(Permissive alternative form)

   WM — This is in allusion to the
traditional P referred to in your Obl,
implying that as a man of honour a FC
FM would rather have his h t f his bt —
illustrates and ensures Can copies —
than improperly disclose the secrets

‖ entrusted to him.

(Continue for either form)

WM — The G or Tn is given — *takes Can's r h and adjusts g by placing Can's t in position before placing his own — by a d* p o t t o t s j o t h. This G or Tn demands a word, a word to be given with the same strict caution as that in the former degree; that is to say, never at length, but always by ls or ss, to enable you to do which I must tell you that the word is ......

SD *repeats word aloud and ensures Can repeats it aloud after him.*

WM *spells word.*

SD *spells word aloud and ensures Can spells it aloud after him.*

WM *retaining g* — As in the course of the ceremony you will be called on for this word the SD will now dictate the answers you are to give. What is this?

SD *prompting Can aloud* — The G or Tn of a FC FM *(Can repeats)*.

WM — What does it demand?

SD *prompting Can aloud* — A word *(Can repeats)*.

WM — Give me that word.

SD *prompting Can aloud (if necessary by phrases) and quickly to prevent him giving word at length* — I was taught to be cautious in this Degree as well as in the former. I will letter or halve it with you *(Can repeats).*

WM — Which you please and begin.

(At this stage the word is halved.)

SD *gives first half (Can repeats).*

WM *gives second half.*

SD *gives complete word (Can repeats).*

WM — This word is derived from the r h p at the p....way or e...e of KST, so named after ......, the Asst H P who officiated at its dedication. The import of the word is, To ......; and when conjoined with that in the former Degree, ..., for God said, 'In ...... I will e this Mine house to stand firm for ever'. Pass, ... — *places r h of Can in l h of SD and sits.*

SD *turns r, controlling Can by holding his r h regains floor of Lodge, turns l, instructs Can in whisper to step off with l f, passes in front of WM's ped to S E corner of Lodge which they 'square'. He leads Can to E side of JW's ped where they stand*

E

parallel to ped and a convenient distance from it and releases h.

SD *rests butt of wand on floor with top resting against r shoulder. Sp and FC Sn* — Bro JW, I present to you Bro ...... on his being passed to the Second Degree — *cuts Sn and takes wand in r h again.*

JW — I will thank Bro ...... to advance to me as a FC.

SD *instructs Can in whisper to take Sp give FC Sn and then to cut Sn, and ensures Can does so.*

JW — Have you anything to communicate?

SD *prompting Can aloud* — I have *(Can repeats).*

JW *rises, faces Can, takes Sp and offers hand.*

SD *places Can's r h in that of JW, adjusting g from above.*

JW *gives g after SD has adjusted Can's r t. (retains g throughout colloquy)* — What is this?

SD *prompting Can aloud* — The G or Tn of a FC FM *(Can repeats).*

JW — What does it demand?

SD *prompting Can aloud* — A word *(Can repeats).*

JW — Give me that word.

SD *prompting Can aloud (quickly and if necessary by phrases).* — I was taught to be cautious in this Degree as well as in the former; I will l or h with you *(Can repeats in similar phrases).*

JW — Which you please, and begin.

(At JW's ped the word is both lettered and halved.)

SD *gives first letter aloud (Can repeats).*

JW *gives second letter.*

SD *gives third letter (Can repeats).*

JW *gives fourth letter.*

SD *gives fifth letter (Can repeats).*

JW *gives last letter.*

SD *gives first half (Can repeats).*

JW *gives second half.*

SD *gives whole word (Can repeats).*

JW — Pass, ... — *replaces Can's r h in l h of SD and sits.*

SD *leads Can via S Wt corner, 'squaring' as before, to S of SW's ped both Can and SD facing N, parallel to SW's ped and a convenient distance from it and* *releases h.*

SD *rests butt of wand on floor with top resting against r shoulder, Sp and FC Sn* — Bro SW, I present to you Bro ...... on his being passed to the Second Degree — *cuts Sn, and takes wand in r h again.*

SW — I will thank Bro ...... to advance to me as a FC, first as an EA.

SD *instructs Can in whisper to take Sp, give EA Sn and cut it and to take second Sp ensuring he does not give FC Sn at this stage.*

SW — What is that?

SD *prompting Can aloud* — The s r sp in Freemasonry *(Can repeats).*

SW — Do you bring anything else?

SD *prompting Can aloud* — I do *(Can repeats).*

SD *instructs Can to give and hold Sn of F and ensures he does so.*

SW — What is that?

SD *prompting Can aloud and by suitable phrases* — The Sn of F, emblematically to shield the repository of my secrets from the attacks of the insidious *(Can repeats).*

SW — Do you bring anything else?

SD *prompting Can aloud* — I do *(Can repeats)*.

SD *instructs Can to give and hold H Sn, and ensures he does so.*

SW — What is that?

SD *prompting Can aloud* — The H Sn or Sn of P *(Can repeats)*.

SW — When did it take its rise?

SD *prompting Can aloud and by suitable phrases* — At the time that J fought the battles of the Lord, when it was in this position he prayed fervently to the Almighty to continue to l of d that he might complete the overthrow of his enemies *(Can repeats)*.

SW — Do you bring anything else?

SD *prompting Can aloud* — I do *(Can repeats)*.

SD *instructs Can to cut both parts of Sn in sequence and ensures he does so.*

SW — What is that?

SD *prompting Can aloud* — The P Sn *(Can repeats)*.

SW — To what does it allude?

SD *prompting Can aloud and by suitable phrases (Can repeating)*.

(Traditional form)

The penalty of my Obl, implying that
as a man of h and a FC FM I would
rather have my h t f m bt — *as Can says
't f m bt' prompts him to give and cut Sn
of F* — than improperly disclose the
secrets entrusted to me.

(Permissive alternative form)

The traditional penalty referred to in
my Obl, implying that as a man of h a
FC FM would rather have his h t f his bt
— *as Can says 't f his bt' prompts him to
give and cut Sn of F* — than improperly
disclose the secrets entrusted to him.

(Continue for either form)

SW — Have you anything to communicate?

SD *prompting Can aloud* — I have *(Can
repeats).*

SW *rises, faces Can, takes Sp and offers
hand.*

SD *places Can's r h in that of SW and
adjusts g from above with l h.*

SW *gives g after SD has adjusted Can's
r t (retains g throughout colloquy)* — What
is this?

SD *prompting Can aloud* — The G or Tn of a FC FM *(Can repeats)*.

SW — What does it demand?

SD *prompting Can aloud* — A word *(Can repeats)*.

SW — Give me that word.

SD *prompting Can aloud (quickly and if necessary by phrases)* — I was taught to be cautious in this Degree as well as in the former; I will letter or halve it with you *(Can repeats)*.

SW — Which you please and begin. *(Here the word is halved.)*

SD *gives first half aloud (Can repeats)*.

SW *gives second half*.

SD *gives whole word (Can repeats)*.

SW — Whence is this word derived?

SD *prompting Can aloud by phrases* — From the r h p at the p...way or e...e of KST, so named after ......, the Asst H P who officiated at its dedication *(Can repeats)*.

SW — The import of the word?

SD *prompting Can aloud* — To ...... *(Can repeats)*.

SW — And what when conjoined with

that in the former Degree?

SD *prompting Can aloud* — ......, for God said — 'In ...... I will e this Mine house to stand firm for ever' *(Can repeats)*.

SW — Pass, ... — *replaces Can's r h in l·h of SD and remains standing.*

SD *takes Can by r h and leads him to N side of SW's ped by passing in front of it. He then makes an anti-clockwise wheel, places Can's r h in l h of SW, and lining up on l·of Can ensures they are both facing E.*

SW *raises Can's r h, Sp and Sn of F.* WM, I present to you Bro ...... on his being passed to the Second Degree for some further mark of your favour.

WM — Bro SW, I delegate you to invest him with the distinguishing badge of a FC FM.

SW *cuts Sn, releases Can's h and with Can facing him puts on him badge of FC FM.*

SD *assists if necessary.*

SW *picks up lower r h corner of badge with his l h; to Can* — Bro ......, by the WM's command I invest you with the distinguishing badge of a FC FM to mark

the progress you have made in the science
— *with his l h restores Can's r h to l h of
SD and sits.*

SD *takes Can's r h from SW, positions
himself on r of Can both facing E and
releases hand.*

WM — Let me add to what has been
stated by the SW that the badge with which
you have now been invested points out that,
as a Cn, you are expected to make the
liberal Arts and Sciences your future study,
that you may the better be enabled to
discharge your duties as a Mason and
estimate the wonderful works of the
Almighty.

WM — Bro SD, you will place our
Brother at the S E part of the Lodge.

SD *takes Can's r h and leads him to S E
part, 'squaring' at NE and SE corners.
Both face N as near as convenient to the
corner of the Lodge. Releases h.*

SD *to Can* — R f across the Lodge, l f
down the Lodge; pay attention to the WM
— *ensures Can forms sq with his ft.*

WM — Masonry being a progressive
science, when you were made an EA you

were placed at the NE part of the Lodge to show that you were newly admitted; you are now placed at the SE part to mark the progress you have made in the science. You now stand to all external appearance a just and upright FC FM, and I give it you in strong terms of recommendation ever to continue and act as such; and as I trust the import of the former charge neither is nor ever will be effaced from your memory, I shall content myself with observing that, as in the previous Degree you made yourself acquainted with the principles of Moral Truth and Virtue, you are now permitted to extend your researches into the hidden mysteries of Nature and Science.

IPM *places w ts in readiness on WM's ped if he has not previously done so.*

SD *takes Can's r h, places him in front of WM in a position as close as convenient to ped from which he can see w ts. Releases h.**

WM — I now present to you the w ts of a FC FM; they are the S, L and PR — *indicates w ts as he names them* — The S is

**See Notes on Ritual and Procedure.*

to try, and adjust rectangular corners of buildings, and assist in bringing rude matter into due form; the L to lay ls and prove horizontals; the PR to try, and adjust uprights while fixing them on their proper bases. But as we are not all operative Masons, but rather free and accepted, or speculative, we apply these ts to our morals. In this sense, the S teaches morality, the L equality, and the PR justness and uprightness of life and actions. Thus by square conduct, level steps, and upright intentions we hope to ascend to those immortal mansions whence all goodness emanates.

WM — You are now at liberty to retire in order to restore yourself to your personal comforts, and on your return to the Lodge I shall call your attention to an explanation of the TB.

SD *takes Can by r h, moves anti-clockwise so as to face W and leads Can directly, no 'squaring', to N of SW's ped. Here he wheels Can clockwise so as to face E, halts and releases hand.*

SD *to Can, aloud* — Salute the WM as a

FC, first as an EA — *instructs Can in whisper to take Sp, give EA Sn and cut it and to take second Sp, give FC Sn and cut it. He ensures Can does so.*

SD *takes Can by r h, makes an anti-clockwise wheel and takes him to door.*

IG *goes to door in front of SD and opens it, closing and locking it again after Can has gone out.*

SD *and* **IG** *resume seats.*

While Can is outside TB is placed on the floor in the C of the Lodge (so as to be viewed from the W) if it is not already situated there.

Outside Lodge Can resumes his ordinary dress with FC badge. When Can is ready, **Tyler** *gives FC ks on door of Lodge.*

IG *rises in front of his chair, Sp and FC Sn* — Bro JW, there is a report — *holds Sn.*

JW *seated, one* ━▪.

IG *cuts Sn, goes to door, opens it and looks out without speaking.*

Tyler — The Can on his return.

IG *makes no reply, closes and locks door and returns to position in front of his chair,*

Sp and FC Sn which he holds. — **WM**, the Can on his return.

WM — Admit him.

IG — *cuts Sn, awaits arrival of SD and then goes to door.*

SD *follows IG to door.*

IG *opens door and admits Can.*

SD *receives Can and leads him by r h to N of SW's ped, both facing E. Releases h.* *

IG, *when SD has received Can, closes and locks door and resumes his seat.*

SD *to Can aloud* — Salute the WM as a FC, first as an EA — *instructs Can to take Sp, give EA Sn and cut it, to take second Sp and give FC Sn and cut it.*

SD *leads Can direct to W side of T B and facing it. Releases h.* *

JD *goes to l side of Can so that all three face E in a line.*

WM *leaves his ped by the left side, goes to the E side of T B.*

JD *hands wand to WM.*

ALL *stand and (except* **Ws** *and* **IG**), *gather round T B.*

---

*See Notes on Ritual and Procedure.

EXPLANATION OF THE SECOND DEGREE TRACING BOARD

**(WM gives the explanation in EL of I).
The various items mentioned in the
explanation may be indicated as appropriate with the butt of the wand.*

When the Temple at Jerusalem was
completed by King Solomon, its costliness
and splendour became objects of ad-
miration to the surrounding nations, and its
fame spread to the remotest parts of the
then known world. There was nothing,
however, in connection with this
magnificent structure more remarkable, or
that more particularly struck the attention,
than the two great Ps which were placed at
the porchway or entrance. That on the l
was called ......, which denotes in ......; that
on the r, ..., which denotes to ......; and
when conjoined ......; for God said 'In I
will e this Mine house to stand firm for
ever.'

The height of those Ps was seventeen

*See Notes on Ritual and Procedure.

cubits and a half each, their circumference twelve, their diameter four. They were formed hollow, the better to serve as archives to Masonry, for therein were deposited the constitutional rolls. Being formed hollow, the outer rim or shell was four inches, or a hand's-breadth, in thickness. They were made of molten brass, and were cast in the plain of Jordan in the clay ground between Succoth and Zeredathah, where King Solomon ordered those and all his holy vessels to be cast. The superintendent of the casting was H A.

Those Ps were adorned with two chapiters, each five cubits high; the chapiters were enriched with network, lily-work and pomegranates. Network, from the connection of its meshes, denotes unity; lily-work, from its whiteness, peace; and pomegranates, from the exuberance of their seed, denote plenty. There were two rows of pomegranates on each chapiter, one hundred in a row. Those Ps were further adorned with two spherical balls on which were delineated maps of the celestial and terrestial globes, pointing out Masonry universal. They were considered finished when the network or canopy was thrown over them.

They were set up as a memorial to the children of Israel of that miraculous pillar of fire and cloud which had two wonderful effects. The fire gave light to the Israelites during their escape from their Egyptian bondage, and the cloud proved darkness to Pharoah and his followers when they attempted to overtake them. King Solomon ordered them to be placed at the entrance of the Temple, as the most proper and conspicuous situation for the children of Israel to have the happy deliverance of their forefathers continually before their eyes in going to and returning from Divine worship.

At the building of KST an immense number of Ms were employed. They consisted of EAs and FCs. The EAs received a weekly allowance of corn, wine and oil; the FCs were paid their wages in specie, which they went to receive in the middle chamber of the Temple. They got there by the p... way or e on the s side.

SECOND DEGREE

After our ancient Brethren had entered the porch, they arrived at the foot of the winding staircase which led to the middle chamber. Their ascent was opposed by the JW, who demanded of them the p g and p w leading from the First to the Second Degree. The p g you are all in possession of, and the p w, I dare say you recollect is ......; ...... denotes ...... and is here depicted by an e o c near to a f o w.

The word ...... dates its origin from the time that an army of Ephraimites crossed the River Jordan in a hostile manner against Jephtha, the renowned Gileaditish general. The reason they assigned for this unfriendly visit was that they had not been called out to partake of the honours of the Ammonitish war, but their true aim was to partake of the rich spoils with which, in consequence of that war, Jephtha and his army were then laden. The Ephraimites had always been considered a clamorous and turbulent people, but then broke out into open violence, and after many severe taunts to the Gileadites in general, threatened to destroy their victorious commander and his house with fire. Jephtha, on his part, tried all lenient means to appease them, but finding these ineffectual had recourse to rigorous ones. He therefore drew out his army, gave the Ephraimites battle, defeated, and put them to flight; and to render his victory decisive, and to secure himself from like molestation in future, he sent detachments of his army to secure the passages of the River Jordan, over which he knew the insurgents must of necessity attempt to go in order to regain their own country, giving strict orders to his guards that if a fugitive came that way, owning himself an Ephraimite, he should immediately be slain; but if he prevaricated, or said 'nay', a test word was to be put to him to pronounce — the word ...... They, from a defect in aspiration peculiar to their dialect, could not pronounce it properly but called it ......, which small variation discovered their country and cost them their lives. And Scripture informs us that there fell on that day, on the field of battle and on the banks of the Jordan, forty and two thousand Ephraimites; and as ......

was then a test word to distinguish friend
from foe, KS afterwards caused it to be
adopted as a p w in a FCs' Lodge to
prevent any unqualified person ascending
the winding staircase which led to the
middle chamber of the Temple.

After our ancient Brethren had given
those convincing proofs to the JW, he said
'Pass, ...' They then passed up the
winding staircase, consisting of three, five,
seven, or more steps. Three rule a Lodge,
five hold a Lodge, seven or more make it
perfect. The three who rule a Lodge are the
Master and his two Wardens; the five who
hold a Lodge are the Master, two Wardens
and two FCs; the seven who make it perfect
are two EAs added to the former five.
Three rule a Lodge because there were but
three Grand Masters who bore sway at the
building of the first T at J, namely S K of I,
H K of T, and HA. Five hold a Lodge in
allusion to the five noble orders of
architecture, namely the Tuscan, Doric,
Ionic, Corinthian and Composite. Seven or
more make a perfect Lodge, because K S
was seven years and upwards in building,

completing, and dedicating the T at J to God's service. They have likewise a further allusion to the seven liberal Arts and Sciences, namely Grammar, Rhetoric, Logic, Arithmetic, Geometry, Music and Astronomy.

After our ancient Brethren had gained the summit of the winding staircase, they arrived at the door of the middle chamber which they found open, but properly tyled against all under the Degree of a FC by the SW, who demanded of them the Sn, Tn and Wd of a FC. After they had given him those convincing proofs he said 'Pass, ...' They then passed into the middle chamber of the Temple, where they went to receive their wages, which they did without scruple or diffidence: without scruple, well knowing they were justly entitled to them, and without diffidence, from the great reliance they placed on the integrity of their employers in those days.

When our ancient Brethren were in the middle chamber of the Temple their attention was peculiarly drawn to certain Hebrew characters which are here depicted by the letter G,

A PM *one* ━┫ **SW** *one* ━┫ **JW** *one*
━┫ .

WM — denoting God — **ALL**, *Sn of R*
— the Grand Geometrician of the
Universe, to whom we must all submit and
whom we ought humbly to adore.

ALL *drop Sn of R.*

WM *restores wand to JD and returns to
his seat by N side.*

JD *returns to his seat.*

SD *leads Can direct to a seat and
returns to his seat.*

ALL *sit.*

THIRD DEGREE
OR
CEREMONY OF RAISING

QUESTIONS BEFORE RAISING

The Lodge is open in the Second Degree.

WM *requests FCs other than Can to withdraw and indicates with appropriate words that the next business is to raise Bro ....*

SD *goes to Can, takes him by r h, leads him to position N of SW's ped, both facing E, and releases h.*

WM — Brethren, Bro ...... is this evening a Can to be raised to the Third Degree, but it is first requisite that he give proofs of proficiency in the Second. I shall therefore proceed to put the necessary questions — *to Can* — How were you prepared to be passed to the Second Degree?

SD *must be prepared, if necessary, to prompt Can.*

Can — In a manner somewhat similar to the former, save that in this Degree I was not h w, my l a, b and r k were made b and my l h was s s.

WM — On what were you admitted?

Can — The sq.

WM — What is a sq?

Can — An angle of ...... dgs, or the f p of a c.

WM — What are the peculiar objects of research in this Degree?

Can — The hidden mysteries of Nature and Science.

WM — As it is the hope of reward that sweetens labour, where did our ancient brethren go to receive their wages?

Can — Into the m c of K S T.

WM — How did they receive them?

Can — Without scruple or diffidence.

WM — Why in this peculiar manner?

Can — Without scruple, well knowing they were justly entitled to them, and without diffidence, from the great reliance they placed on the integrity of their employers in those days.

WM — What were the names of the two great Ps which were placed at the p...way or e of K S T ?

Can — That on the l was called ......, and

that on the r ......

WM — What are their separate and conjoint significations?

Can — The former denotes in ......, the latter to ......; and when conjoined ......, for God said, 'In ...... I will establish this Mine house to stand firm for ever.'

WM — These are the usual questions; I will put others if any Brother wishes me to do so.

SD *conducts Can by r h direct to N side of WM's ped and a convenient distance from it, both facing S and releases h.*

WM — Do you pledge your honour as a man and your fidelity as a Craftsman that you will steadily persevere through the ceremony of being raised to the sublime Degree of a MM?

SD *prompting Can aloud* — I do *(Can repeats).*

(For Lodges using traditional form of obl.)

WM — Do you likewise pledge yourself, under the penalty of both your Obls, that you will conceal what I shall now impart to you with the same strict

caution as the other secrets in Masonry?
(For Lodges using permissive alternative form of obl.)

WM — Do you likewise pledge yourself that you will conceal what I shall now impart to you with the same strict caution as the other secrets in Masonry? *(Continue for either form.)*

SD *prompting Can aloud* — I do *(Can repeats).*

WM — Then I will entrust you with a test of merit, which is a p g and p w leading to the Degree to which you seek to be admitted — *rises, faces Can, and takes the latter's r h in his own r h and holds it.* — The p g is given by a d p o t t b t s a t js o t h — *adjusts p g by placing Can's t in position before placing his own* — This p g demands a p w, which is ....

SD *prompting Can, speaks word aloud (Can repeats).*

WM .... was the first a in ms. The import of the word is .... You must be particularly careful to remember this word as without it you cannot gain admission into a Lodge in a superior degree. Pass, ...

...... — *restores Can's r h to l h of S D and sits.*

SD *guiding Can, makes a clockwise wheel and conducts him direct to N of SW's ped. Here he wheels Can clockwise so as to face E and releases h.*

SD *to Can aloud* — Salute the WM as a FC, first as an EA — *instructs Can in a whisper to take Sp, give EA Sn and cut it; take another Sp and give FC Sn and cut it.*

SD *takes Can by r h, makes anti-clockwise wheel with Can and conducts him to door.*

IG *goes to door in front of S D and opens it, closing and locking it again when Can has gone out.*

IG *and* **SD** *return to seats.*

THE RAISING

WM *conducts Opening the Lodge in Third Degree or Resumes in that Degree whichever is appropriate. This will conclude with*

*WM *MM* ⊸ *quietly (ie, given so as to be audible only in the Lodge).*

*See Notes on Ritual and Procedure.

*SW *MM* ——▪ *quietly* **JW** *MM* ——▪ *quietly.*

*TB *is attended to when JW has given ks (usually by* **JD**).

*IG *gives ks by r h on l sleeve, standing in his place.*

IPM, *meanwhile, exposes both ps of Cs.* (No ks are given on door by either IG or Tyler).*

Ds *lay down and open s.*

Tyler *prepares Can including FC badge and Ceremony proceeds —*

Tyler *gives FC ks on door. This informs Lodge that a Can for Raising is at the door of the Lodge.*

IG *rises in front of his chair, Sp and MM P Sn —* Bro J W, there is a report — *holds Sn.*

JW *no ks, rises, Sp and MM P Sn —* WM, there is a report — *holds Sn.*

WM — Bro JW, inquire who wants admission.

JW *cuts Sn and recovers, and sits —* Bro IG, see who wants admission.

IG *cuts Sn and recovers, goes to door,*

*See Notes on Ritual and Procedure.

*opens it, checks that Can is properly pre-
pared, and remains on threshold with hand
on door handle (Colloquy between IG and
Tyler should be audible throughout Lodge).*

IG, *to Tyler* — Whom have you there?

Tyler *names Can* — Bro ...... who has
been regularly initiated into Freemasonry,
passed to the Degree of a FC, and has
made such further progress as he hopes will
entitle him to be raised to the sublime
Degree of a MM, for which ceremony he is
properly prepared.

IG — How does he hope to obtain the
privileges of the Third Degree?

Tyler — By the help of God, the united
aid of the S and Cs, and the benefit of a
p w.

IG — Is he in possession of the p w?

Tyler — Will you prove him?

IG *receives p g and p w from Can* (**Tyler**
prompts if necessary).

IG — Halt, while I report to the WM —
*closes and locks door, returns to position in
front of his chair, Sp and MM P Sn which
he holds.*

IG — WM — *names Can* — Bro ......,

who has been regularly initiated into Freemasonry, passed to the degree of a FC, and
has made such further progress as he hopes
will entitle him to be raised to the sublime
Degree of a MM, for which ceremony he is
properly prepared.

WM — How does he hope to obtain the
privileges of the Third Degree?

IG — By the help of God, the united aid
of the S and Cs, and the benefit of a p w.

WM — We acknowledge the powerful
aid by which he seeks admission; do you,
Bro IG, vouch that he is in possession of
the p w?

IG — I do, WM.

WM — Then let him be admitted in due
form.

IG *cuts Sn and recovers.*

WM — Bro Deacons.

JD *places kneeling stool in position.*

IG *takes Cs and goes to door followed by*
JD *and* **SD**, *SD on left.*

*It is at this point that all ls except that of
the WM are extinguished.*

IG *opens door, retaining hold on it as
before, applies extended Cs to both bs of*

Can and then raises Cs above his head to show that he has so applied them.

SD *with l h takes Can by r h* (**JD** *on Can's l*) *leads him to kneeling stool, two short paces from it and releases h. All three stand facing E.*

IG *after Can is admitted closes and locks door and resumes his seat.*

SD *to Can* — Advance as a FC, first as an EA — *ensures that Can takes Sp and gives and cuts EA Sn, then takes second Sp and gives and cuts FC Sn.*

WM — Let the Can kneel while the blessing of Heaven is invoked on what we are about to do.

SD *ensures Can kneels and gives Sn of R.*

WM *one* ⊣ **SW** *one* ⊣ **JW** *one* ⊣.

Ds *hold wands in l h cross them over head of Can and give Sn of R.*

ALL *stand with Sn of R.*

PRAYER

*(**WM** *says prayer in E L of I.*)
Almighty and Eternal God, Architect
See Notes on Ritual and Procedure.

and Ruler of the Universe, at Whose creative fiat all things first were made, we, the frail creatures of Thy providence, humbly implore Thee to pour down on this convocation assembled in Thy Holy Name the continual dew of Thy blessing. Especially, we beseech Thee to impart Thy grace to this Thy servant, who offers himself a Candidate to partake with us the mysterious Scts of a MM. Endue him with such fortitude that in the hour of trial he fail not, but that, passing safely under Thy protection through the valley of the shadow of death, he may finally rise from the tomb of transgression, to shine as the stars for ever and ever.

*IPM — So mote it be.

ALL drop Sn of R.

Ds *uncross wands and hold them again in r h.*

WM — Let the Candidate rise (*He does so*).

WM *sits.*

ALL (*except* **Ds** *and* **Can**) *sit.*

JD *draws kneeling stool aside to his left*

**See Notes on Ritual and Procedure.*

out of way of SD and Can.

SD *takes Can's r h firmly, instructs him in a whisper to step off with l f and leads Can up N towards E part of Lodge.*

JD *follows close behind Can and continues to do so for complete perambulation.*

IG *replaces kneeling stool in normal position.*

SD *leads Can to N E corner where they 'square' Lodge (SD should ensure that when 'squaring' sufficient space is left for JD behind SD and Can*); SD instructs Can to step off with l f and proceeds with him (JD following) to point in front of WM's ped, halts there and releases h.*

SD *to Can* — Salute the WM as a Mason — *ensures Can takes Sp, gives EA Sn and cuts it.*

SD *takes Can by r h, instructs him to step off with l f and leads him via S E corner which is 'squared' to E side of JW's ped where they stand parallel to ped and a convenient distance from it. Releases h.*

JD *stands as nearly behind Can as is possible.*

**See Notes on Ritual and Procedure.*

SD — Advance to the JW as such, showing the Sn and communicating the Tn and Wd — *ensures Can takes Sp and gives EA Sn and cuts it.*

JW — Have you anything to communicate?

SD *prompting Can aloud* — I have *(Can repeats).*

JW *rises, faces Can with Sp and offers hand.*

SD *places r h of Can in that of JW and adjusts EA g from above.*

JW *gives g after SD has adjusted Can's r t and retains g throughout the whole of the colloquy* — What is this?

SD *prompting Can aloud* — The G or Tn of an EA FM *(Can repeats).*

JW — What does it demand?

SD *prompting Can aloud* — A word *(Can repeats).*

JW — Give me that word freely and at length.

SD *prompting Can aloud* — ...... *(Can repeats).*

JW — Pass, ... — *replaces Can's r h in l h of SD and sits.*

F

SD *leads Can on to floor of Lodge, instructs him to step off with l f and leads him via S Wt corner which is 'squared' to a point in front of SW's ped, halts and releases hand.*

SD — Salute the SW as a Mason — *ensures Can takes Sp, gives EA Sn and cuts it.*

SD *takes Can's r h, instructs him to step off with l f, leads him to N W corner of Lodge which is 'squared' and proceeds with Can towards E end of Lodge to perambulate a second time.*

JD *continues to follow close behind Can on this perambulation.*

SD *leads Can to N E corner of Lodge which is 'squared' and on to point in front of WM's ped, halts there and releases h.*

SD — Salute the WM as a FC — *ensures Can takes Sp, gives FC Sn and cuts it.*

SD *takes Can's r h, instructs him to step off with l f and leads him via S E corner which is 'squared' to a point in front of JW's ped, halts, and releases h.*

SD *to Can* — Salute the JW as a FC —

ensures Can takes Sp, gives FC Sn and cuts it.

SD *takes Can's r h instructs him to step off with l f and leads him via S Wt corner which is 'squared' to S side of SW's ped where they stand parallel to ped and a convenient distance from it. Releases h.**

JD *stands as nearly behind Can as possible.*

SD — Advance to the SW as such, showing the Sn and communicating the Tn and Wd of that Degree — *ensures Can takes Sp, gives FC Sn and cuts it.*

SW — Have you anything to communicate?

SD *prompting Can aloud* — I have *(Can repeats).*

SW — *rises, faces Can with Sp and offers hand.*

SD *places r h of Can in that of SW and adjusts FC g from above.*

SW *gives g after SD has adjusted Can's r t and retains g throughout the whole of the colloquy.*

SW — What is this?

*See Notes on Ritual and Procedure.

SD *prompting Can aloud* — The G or Tn of a FC FM *(Can repeats)*.

SW — What does it demand?

SD *prompting Can aloud* — A word *(Can repeats)*.

SW — Give me that word, freely and at length.

SD *prompting Can aloud* — ..... *(Can repeats)*.

SW — Pass, ... — *replaces Can's r h in l h of SD and sits.*

SD *takes Can's r h and leads him on to floor of Lodge, instructs him to step off with l f and leads him to N of SW's ped, wheels clockwise so that both face WM and releases h.*

JD *follows Can till SD and Can face WM, then passes behind them and stands on l of Can so that all three are in line facing E.*

WM one ➝ **SW** one ➝ **JW** one ➝.

WM — The Brethren will take notice that Bro ......, who has been regularly initiated into Freemasonry and passed to the Degree of a FC, is about to pass in view

before them, to show that he is the Can
properly prepared to be raised to the
sublime Degree of a MM.

SD *takes Can's r h, instructs him to step
off with l f and leads him up N side of
Lodge to perambulate a third time.*

JD *falls in behind Can as on previous
perambulations and again continues to
follow close behind Can.*

SD *leads Can to NE corner which is
'squared' and proceeds to point in front of
WM's ped, halts and releases h.*

SD — Salute the WM as a FC —
*ensures Can takes Sp, gives FC Sn and
cuts it.*

SD *takes Can's r h, continues
perambulation, 'squaring' S E corner, halts
in front of JW's ped and releases h.**

SD — Salute the JW as a FC — *ensures
Can takes Sp, gives FC Sn and cuts it.*

SD *takes Can's r h instructs him to step
off with l f and continues permabulation,
'squaring' S Wt corner and leads Can to S
of SW's ped, standing parallel to ped and a
convenient distance from it. Releases h.*

*See Notes on Ritual and Procedure.

SD — Advance to the SW as such, showing the Sn and communicating the p g and p w you received from the WM previously to leaving the Lodge — *ensures Can takes Sp, gives FC Sn and cuts it.*

SW — Have you anything to communicate?

SD *prompting Can aloud* — I have *(Can repeats).*

SW *rises, faces Can and offers hand.*

SD *places Can's r h in that of SW and with l h adjusts p g from above.*

SW *gives p g after SD has adjusted Can's r t and retains p g throughout colloquy.*

SW — What is this?

SD *prompting Can aloud* — The p g leading from the Second to the Third Degree *(Can repeats).*

SW — What does this p g demand?

SD *prompting Can aloud* — A p w *(Can repeats).*

SW — Give me that p w.

SD *prompting Can aloud* — .... *(Can repeats).*

SW — What was ....?

SD *prompting Can aloud* — The first a in ms *(Can repeats)*.

SW — The import of the word?

SD *prompting Can aloud* — .... *(Can repeats)*.

SW — Pass, ... — *replaces Can's r h in l h of SD and remains standing.*

SD *takes Can's r h and leads him on to floor of Lodge, instructs him to step off with l f and leads him to N side of SW's ped. Here he makes an anti-clockwise wheel and places Can's r h in l h of SW; he lines up on l of Can and ensures that both are facing E.*

JD *follows Can and as SD and Can wheel continues on and takes up position on l of SD so that all three are in line, facing E.*

SW *holding up Can's r h Sp and MM P Sn* — WM, I present to you Bro ......, a Can properly prepared to be raised to the Third Degree — *maintains Sn and continues to hold Can's r h.*

WM — Bro SW, you will direct the Ds to instruct the Can to advance to the E by the proper sps.

SW *cuts Sn and recovers, replaces Can's*

r h in l h of SD and sits.

SD *takes up a position on r of Can, ensures that both face E and releases h.*

JD *remains in position, now on l of Can.*

SW — Bro Ds, it is the WM's command that you instruct the Can to advance to the E by the proper sps.

SD *takes Can's r h, instructs him to step off with l f and leads him up N side of Lodge to a convenient point opposite s, halts and turns with him to face S.*

JD *follows close behind Can and when SD halts passes behind Can and turns S so that all three are in line.*

SD *leaves Can and goes, by passing outside W end of s, to far side of s from Can, turns and halts facing him.*

SD *to Can* — The method of advancing from W to E in this degree is by ...., the first ...... as if stepping over a g. For your information I will go through them, and you will afterwards copy me.

SD *goes to hd or W end of g and stands facing E, ft formed in a sq h to h, l f pointing E and r f pointing S. Commencing with l f, he takes a Sp across the g in a N E* *direction, the l f being placed at the N side of the g about one-third of the latter's length and pointing N. The Sp is completed by bringing the r f up to the l f, h to h in the f o a s and with the r f pointing E. Commencing with the r f, he takes a second Sp across the g in a S E direction, the r f being placed at the S side of the g about two-thirds of the latter's length and pointing S. This Sp is completed by bringing the l f up to the r f h to h in the f o a s, the l f pointing E. Commencing with the l f he takes a third Sp to the foot or E end of the g, the l f pointing E. The Sp is completed by bringing up the r f to the l f, h to h in the f o a s and r f pointing S. Commencing with the l f he takes f...r Sps in a direction due E, finishing in front of WM's ped with the ft h to h in the f o a s, l f pointing N E and r f pointing S E.*

SD *then returns to Can, going via the S and W of the s, takes him by r h, places him in position at W end of g and keeping ahead of him, on S side of g instructs him in a whisper how to take Sps, pointing out position for Can's ft. He does not retain* handclasp. When Can reaches E end of g at t...d Sp, SD walks beside him for last f...r Sps and remains on his r in front of WM's ped.

JD *remains stationary while Can is taking first t Sps and then moves so as to arrive at WM's ped simultaneously with SD and Can and takes position on l of Can so that all three are in line facing E.*

WM — It is but fair to inform you that a most serious trial of your fortitude and fidelity and a more solemn Obl await you. Are you prepared to meet them as you ought?

Can — I am *(If Can does not answer* **SD** *should whisper to him 'Answer').*

WM — Then you will k on b ks, place b hs on the VSL *(Can does so). WM ensures Can does not place h on S and Cs.*

WM *one* ➡❘ **SW** *one* ➡❘ **JW** *one* ➡❘ .

ALL *rise with Sp and MM P Sn.*

Ds *hold wands in l h, cross them over head of Can, Sp and MM P Sn.*

WM, *to Can* — Repeat your name at length, and say after me:

I, ... — *Can gives name in full* — in the presence of the Most High, and of this worthy and worshipful Lodge of MMs, duly constituted, regularly assembled, and properly dedicated, of my own free will and accord, do hereby — *with l h touches one or both hs of Can* — and hereon — *with l h touches VSL* — most solemnly promise and swear that I will always h* (*pronounced hail*) conceal, and never reveal any or either of the secrets or mysteries of or belonging to the Degree of a MM to anyone in the world, unless it be to him or them to whom the same may justly and lawfully belong, and not even to him or them until after due trial, strict examination, or full conviction that he or they are worthy of that confidence, or in the body of a MMs' Lodge duly opened on the C.

I further solemnly pledge myself to adhere to the principles of the S and Cs, answer and obey all lawful Sns, and summonses sent to me from a MMs' Lodge, if within the length of my c t, and

See Notes on Ritual and Procedure.

plead no excuse, except sickness or the pressing emergencies of my own public or private avocations.

I further solemnly engage myself to maintain and uphold the f p o f in act as well as in word: that my hand, given to a MM, shall be a sure pledge of brotherhood; that my feet shall travel through dangers and difficulties to unite with his in forming a column of mutual defence and support; that the posture of my daily supplications shall remind me of his wants, and dispose my heart to succour his weakness and relieve his necessities, so far as may fairly be done without detriment to myself or connections; that my breast shall be the sacred repository of his secrets when entrusted to my care — murder, treason, felony, and all other offences contrary to the laws of God and the ordinances of the realm being at all times most especially excepted.

And finally, that I will maintain a MM's honour and carefully preserve it as my own: I will not injure him myself, or knowingly suffer it to be done by others if in my power to prevent it, but, on the contrary, will boldly repel the slanderer of his good name, and most strictly respect the chastity of those nearest and dearest to him, in the persons of his wife, his sister and his child.

All these points I solemnly swear to observe, without evasion, equivocation or mental reservation of any kind,

(Traditional form.)

under no less a penalty, on the violation of any of them, than that of being s i t, m b b t as, and t as s over t f o e and w b t f c w o h, that no trace or remembrance of so vile a wretch may longer be found among men, particularly MMs.

(Permissive alternative form.)

ever bearing in mind the traditional penalty on the violation of any of them, that of being s i t the b b t as and t as s over t f o e and w b t f c w o h, that no trace or remembrance of so vile a wretch may longer be found among men, particularly MMs.

(Continue for either form.)

So help me the Most High, and keep me steadfast in this my solemn Obl of a MM.

ALL *cut P Sn and recover.*

Ds *lower wands to r h.*

WM — As a pledge of your fidelity, and to render this binding as a SO for so long as you shall live, you will s i w y ls th on the VSL *(Can does so).*

SD *if necessary instructs in a whisper.*

WM — Let me once more call your attention to the position of the S and Cs. When you were made an EA both points were hid; in the Second Degree one was disclosed; in this the whole is exhibited implying that you are now at liberty to work with both those points in order to render the circle of your Masonic duties complete.

WM *takes Can's r h from VSL with his r h* — Rise newly obligated MM — *restores Can's r h to SD.*

WM *sits.*

ALL*(except* **Ds** *and Can)sit.*

Ds, *assisting Can, if necessary by taking his hs, step backwards with him till standing at ft of g and there halt in line still facing E.*

THE EXHORTATION

WM — Having entered upon the SO of a MM, you are now entitled to demand that last and greatest trial by which alone you can be admitted to a participation of the secrets of this Degree; but it is first my duty to call your attention to a retrospect of those degrees in Freemasonry through which you have already passed, that you may the better be enabled to distinguish and appreciate the connection of our whole system, and the relative dependency of its several parts.

Your admission among Masons in a state of helpless indigence was an emblematical representation of the entrance of all men on this, their mortal existence. It inculcated the useful lessons of natural equality and mutual dependence; it instructed you in the active principles of universal beneficence and charity, to seek the solace of your own distress by extending relief and consolation to your fellow-creatures in the hour of their affliction. Above all, it taught you to bend with humility and resignation to the will of the Great Architect of the Universe; to dedicate your heart, thus purified from every baneful and malignant passion, fitted only for the reception of truth and wisdom, to His glory and the welfare of your fellow-mortals.

Proceeding onwards, still guiding your progress by the principles of moral truth, you were led in the Second Degree to contemplate the intellectual faculty and to trace it from its development, through the paths of heavenly science, even to the throne of God Himself. The secrets of Nature and the principles of intellectual truth were then unveiled to your view. To your mind, thus modelled by virtue and science, Nature, however, presents one great and useful lesson more. She prepares you, by contemplation, for the closing hour of existence; and when by means of that contemplation she has conducted you through the intricate windings of this mortal life, she finally instructs you how to die.

Such, my Brother, are the peculiar

objects of the Third Degree in Free-masonry. They invite you to reflect on this awful subject, and teach you to feel that, to the just and virtuous man, death has no terrors equal to the stain of falsehood and dishonour. Of this great truth the annals of Masonry afford a glorious example in the unshaken fidelity and noble death of our Master H A, who was slain just before the completion of K S T, at the construction of which he was, as no doubt you are well aware, the principal Architect. The manner of his death was as follows.

WM *calls Ws* — Bro Ws.

Ws *leave their seats; SW by N side taking L with him, JW by W side taking PR with him. SW proceeds eastwards straight up the Lodge; JW waits until SW is level with him and then both advance abreast until they arrive behind the Ds. SW touches JD's r shoulder and JW, simultaneously, touches SD's l shoulder.*

Ds *step one pace outwards.*

Ws *come up in line between Ds and the Can, SW on l and JW on r of Can. This line of five is held momentarily from N to S,* *facing E.*

Ds *then turn outwards and return to their seats.*

JW *directs Can to cross r f over l.*

Ws *hold Can securely by his hs so that they have full control over him and he does not at any time lose his balance.*

WM — Fifteen FCs, of that superior class appointed to preside over the rest, finding that the work was nearly completed and that they were not in possession of the secrets of the Third Degree, conspired to obtain them by any means, even to have recourse to violence. At the moment, however, of carrying their conspiracy into execution, twelve of the fifteen recanted; but three, of a more determined and atrocious character than the rest, persisted in their impious design, in the prosecution of which they planted themselves respectively at the E, N, and S entrances of the Temple, whither our M⸳⸳⸳ retired to pay his adoration to the MH, as was his wonted custom at the hour of high twelve. Having finished his devotions, he attempted to return by the S entrance, where he was opposed by the first of those ruffians, who, for want of other weapon, had armed himself with a heavy P R, and in a threatening manner demanded the secrets of a MM, warning him that death would be the consequence of a refusal. Our Master, true to his Obl, answered that those secrets were known to but ...... in the world and that without the consent and co-operation of the other ...... he neither could nor would divulge them, but intimated that he had no doubt patience and industry would, in due time, entitle the worthy M to a participation of them, but that, for his own part, he would rather suffer death than betray the sacred trust reposed in him.

This answer not proving satisfactory, the ruffian aimed a violent blow at the head of our M; but being startled at the firmness of his demeanour, it missed his forehead and only glanced on his r temple — **JW** *touches Can's r t with P R (the movement may be made from front to back)* — but with such force as to cause him to reel and sink on his l k.

SW *in whisper instructs Can to k on l k*

and then to regain upright position; Ws assist and ensure Can recrosses ft.

WM — Recovering from the shock he made for the N entrance where he was accosted by the second of those ruffians, to whom he gave a similar answer with undiminished firmness, when the ruffian, who was armed with a L, struck him a violent blow on the l temple — **SW** *touches Can on l temple with L* — which brought him to the ground on his r k.

SW *in whisper instructs Can to k on r k and then to regain upright position; Ws assist and ensure Can recrosses ft.*

WM — Finding his retreat cut off at both those pts, he staggered, faint and bleeding, to the E entrance where the third ruffian was posted, who received a similar answer to his insolent demand, for even at this trying moment our M remained firm and unshaken, when the villain, who was armed with a heavy Ml, struck him a violent blow on the forehead — *seated, lifts heavy Ml and goes through movement of striking without touching Can* — which laid him lifeless at his feet.

Ws *lower Can backwards to supine position, with arms at sides and r f still crossed over l f.*

Ws *stand on each side of Can at head of g facing E, JW on S side.*

WM — The Brethren will take notice that in the recent ceremony, as well as in his present situation, our Brother has been made to represent one of the brightest characters recorded in the annals of Masonry, namely H A, who lost his life in consequence of his unshaken fidelity to the sacred trust reposed in him, and I hope this will make a lasting impression on his and your minds should you ever be placed in a similar state of trial.

Brother JW, you will endeavour to raise the representative of our M by the EA's G.

JW *proceeds on r side of Can to level of Can's knees, steps across him with his r f, lifts Can's r h with his l h, gives EA g with his r h, slips it, and with l h gently replaces Can's r h to his side. He returns to his former position at head of g.*

JW *Sp and MM P Sn* — WM, it proves a ...... — *cuts Sn and recovers.*

WM — Brother SW, you will try the FC's.

SW *proceeds on l side of Can to level of Can's knees, steps across him with his l f, lifts Can's r h with his l h, gives FC g with his r h, slips it and with l h gently replaces Can's r h to his side. He returns to his former position at head of g.*

SW *Sp and MM P Sn* — WM, it proves a ..... likewise — *cuts Sn and recovers.*

WM — Brother Ws, having both failed in your attempts, there remains a third method, by taking a more firm h of the sinews of the h and raising him on the F P O F, which with your assistance. I will make trial of — *leaves chair by S, advances to feet of Can which he uncrosses, so that heels are about 6 inches apart. WM then puts r f to r f, takes Can's r h by MM g, and with the aid of the Ws..... Can on the F P O F.*

SW *ensures Can's l h is extended over WM's shoulder, palm downwards, t in f o a s.*

WM *in h o b position* — It is thus all MMs are ..... from a figurative ..... to a reunion with the former companions of their toils — *disengages* — Brother Ws, resume your seats.

Ws *return direct to seats and replace L and P R.*

WM *takes Can by both hs and gently moves him round clockwise so that he stands in the N facing S. WM places Can's hs at his sides, steps backwards beyond the line of g and halts there. WM and Can are now directly facing each other.*

THE CHARGE

WM *to Can* — Let me now beg you to observe that the Light of a MM is darkness visible, serving only to express that gloom which rests on the prospect of futurity. It is that mysterious veil which the eye of human reason cannot penetrate, unless assisted by that Light which is from above. Yet, even by this glimmering ray, you may perceive that you stand on the very b of the g into which you have just figuratively descended, and which, when this transitory life shall have passed away, will again receive you into its cold bosom. Let the emblems of mortality which lie before you lead you to contemplate on your inevitable destiny, and guide your reflections to that most interesting of all human studies, the knowledge of your self. Be careful to perform your allotted task while it is yet day. Continue to listen to the voice of Nature, which bears witness that even in this perishable frame resides a vital and immortal principle, which inspires a holy confidence that the Lord of Life will enable us to trample the King of Terrors beneath our feet, and lift our eyes to that bright Morning Star, whose rising brings peace and salvation to the faithful and obedient of the human race — *steps forward, takes both hs of Can, and gently moves round anti-clockwise until they have exchanged places. Can is now in the S facing N, about three short paces from centre line of Lodge.*

WM — I cannot better reward the attention you have paid to this exhortation and charge than by entrusting you with the secrets of the Degree. You will therefore advance to me as a FC, first as an EA — *ensures Can takes Sp, gives EA Sn and* *cuts it, takes another Sp, gives FC Sn and cuts it* — You will now take another short pace towards me with your l f, bringing the r h into its h as before. That is the t r sp in Freemasonry, and it is in this position that the secrets of the Degree are communicated. They consist of Sns, a Tn and Wd.

Of the Sns, the first and second are casual, the third penal. The first casual Sn is called the Sn of H, and is given from the FC's. — Stand to order as a FC — *ensures Can gives FC Sn and holds it, then himself takes Sp and gives FC Sn* — by dropping the l h i t p, e t r w t h i o t r s, as if struck with h at some d a a s — *illustrates as words require and ensures Can copies.*

The second casual Sn is called the Sn of S, and is given by bending the h f a smg t f g w t r h — *illustrates as words require and ensures Can copies.*

Place your h in this position with t t e i t f o a s — *illustrates and ensures Can copies* — The P S is given b d t h s a t b, d i t t s, a r w t t t t n. — *illustrates as words require and ensures Can copies.*

(Traditional Form.)

This is in allusion to the p of your Obl, implying that as a man of honour and a MM, you would rather be s i t — *illustrates with recovery and ensures Can copies* — than improperly disclose the secrets entrusted to you.

(Permissive alternative form.)

This is in allusion to the traditional p referred to in your Obl, implying that as a man of honour, a MM would rather be s i t — *illustrates with recovery and ensures Can copies* — than improperly disclose the secrets entrusted to him.

(Continue for either form.)

The G or Tn is the first of the f p o f. They are — *illustrates each with Can as words require and ensures Can's correct co-operation* — *h to h, f to f, k to k, b to b, and h over b — *disengages, placing ft to order (Can copies)* — and may be thus briefly explained.

WM *illustrates during explanation again with Can as words require and ensures Can's correct co-operation* — h to h, I greet you as a Brother; f to f, I will support you

*See Notes on Ritual and Procedure.

in all your laudable undertakings; k to k, the posture of my daily supplications shall remind me of your wants ; b to b, your lawful secrets when entrusted to me as such I will keep as my own; and h over b, I will support your character in your absence as in your presence. It is in this position, and this only, and then only in a ......, except in open Lodge, that the word is given: it is ...... or ...... — *speaks words aloud while still holding last of f p o f with Can, ensures Can repeats words aloud, then disengages, standing facing Can.*

WM — You are now at liberty to retire in order to restore yourself to your personal comforts, and on your return to the Lodge the Sns, Tn and Wd, will be further explained — *resumes seat by N side.*

SD *goes to Can and with his l h takes Can's r h and leads him direct (via N side of L avoiding g) to N of SW's ped. Here he wheels Can clockwise so as to face E, halts and releases h.*

SD *to Can aloud* — Salute the WM in the three Degrees — *whispers to Can 'P Sn only in the Third' and ensures Can gives* *the three Sns in order with proper Sps.*

SD *takes Can by r h, makes anti-clockwise wheel and leads him to door.*

IG *goes to door in front of SD and opens it, closing and locking it again after Can has gone out.*

The ls are now restored.

SD *and* **IG** *resume seats.*

Ds *take up s.*

Outside Lodge Can resumes his ordinary dress with FC badge. When Can is ready **Tyler** *gives MM ks on door of Lodge.*

IG *rises in front of his chair, Sp and MM P Sn*— Bro JW, there is a report.

JW *seated on* ➤🯂.

IG *cuts Sn and recovers, goes to door, opens it and looks out without speaking.*

Tyler — The Can on his return.

IG *makes no reply, closes and locks door, returns to position in front of his chair, Sp and MM P Sn which he holds*— WM, the Can on his return.

WM — Admit him.

IG *cuts Sn and recovers, awaits arrival of SD, then goes to door.*

SD *follows IG to door.*

IG *opens door and admits Can.*

SD *receives Can and leads him by r h to N of SW's ped both facing E.*

IG, *when SD has received Can, closes and locks door and resumes his seat.*

SD *to Can aloud* — Salute the WM in the Three Degrees — *whispers 'full Sns' and ensures Can takes Sp and shows and cuts EA Sn, takes second Sp and shows FC Sn without cutting it, takes third Sp while holding FC Sn and gives Sn of H, Sn of S and P Sn including recovery.*

SD *takes Can by r h and draws him back to N of SW.*

SW *rises.*

SD *places Can's r h in l h of SW and lines up on l of Can ensuring they are both facing E.*

SW *with l h raises Can's r h, Sp and MM P Sn* — WM, I present to you Brother ......, on his being raised to the Third Degree, for some further mark of your favour.

WM — Brother SW, I delegate you to invest him with the distinguishing badge of a MM.

SW *cuts Sn and recovers, releases Can's h and with Can facing him puts on him badge of MM.*

SD *assists if necessary.*

SW *picks up lower r h corner of badge with his l h, to Can* — Bro..........., by the WM's command, I invest you with the distinguishing badge of a MM to mark the further progress you have made in the science — *with his l h restores r h of Can to l h of SD and sits.*

SD *takes Can's r h from SW, positions himself on r of Can, both facing E, and releases h.*

WM — I must state that the badge with which you have now been invested not only points out your rank as a MM, but is meant to remind you of those great duties you have just solemnly engaged yourself to observe; and whilst it marks your own superiority, it calls on you to afford assistance and instruction to the brethren in the inferior degrees.

SD *takes Can's r h and leads him direct (no 'squaring') to face WM's ped about a pace away from it. Releases h.*

TRADITIONAL HISTORY

*(**WM** delivers the Traditional history in E L of Imp)*

We left off at that part of our traditional history which mentions the death of our Master H A. A loss so important as that of the principal architect could not fail of being generally and severely felt. The want of those plans and designs which had hitherto been regularly supplied to the different classes of workmen was the first indication that some heavy calamity had befallen our M. The Menatschin, or Prefects, or, more familiarly speaking, the Overseers, deputed some of the most eminent of their number to acquaint K S with the utter confusion into which the absence of H had plunged them, and to express their apprehension that to some fatal catastrophe must be attributed his sudden and mysterious disappearance. K S immediately ordered a general muster of the workmen throughout the different departments, when three of the same class

*See Notes on Ritual and Procedure.

of overseers were not to be found. On the same day the twelve Craftsmen who had originally joined in the conspiracy came before the King and made a voluntary confession of all they knew down to the time of withdrawing themselves from the number of the conspirators. This naturally increased the fears of K S for the safety of his chief artist. He therefore selected fifteen trusty FCs and ordered them to make diligent search after the person of our M, to ascertain if he were yet alive, or had suffered death in the attempt to extort from him the secrets of his exalted Degree.

Accordingly, a stated day having been appointed for their return to Jerusalem, they formed themselves into three FCs' Lodges and departed from the three entrances of the Temple. Many days were spent in fruitless search; indeed, one class returned without having made any discovery of importance. A second, however, were more fortunate, for on the evening of a certain day, after having suffered the greatest privations and personal fatigues, one of the brethren, who

ost fidelity; and on reopening the
und one of the brethren looking round,
rises, no Sp — observed some of his
panions in this p — *gives Sn of H,* **SD**
res Can copies — struck with h at the
ful and afflicting sight — *drops Sn* —
others, viewing the ghastly w still
e on his f, smote their own — *gives Sn*
SD *ensures Can copies* — in
thy with his sufferings — *drops Sn*
its — Two of the brethren then
ed the g and endeavoured to raise
the EA's G which proved a s. They
ed the FC's, which proved a s
. Having both failed in their
, a zealous and expert brother took
irm h o t s o t h, and with their
, raised him on the f p o f, while
ore animated, exclaimed ...... or
words having a nearly similar
e signifying the d of the b, the
b is sm. K S therefore ordered
casual Sns and that Tn and Wd
gnate all MMs, throughout the
il time or circumstances should
enuine.

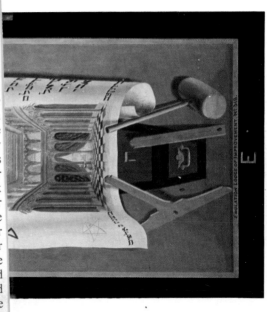

had rested himself in a reclinin
assist his rising caught hold o
grew near, which to his surpri
out of the ground. On a clos
he found that the earth ha
disturbed. He therefo
companions and wit
endeavours reopened the
found the b of our N
interred. They covered
respect and reverence
the spot stuck a sprig
of the grave.

They then haste
impart the afflicting
when the first em
subsided, ordered
our M to such a
rank and exalted
informing them
the secrets of a
charged them
observing wh
might occur
tribute of res

They pe

utr
gro
—
com
ensu
drea
while
visibl
of S
symp
and s
descen
him by
then tr
likewise
attempts
a more
assistanc
others, m
......, both
import, o
other the
that those
should des
universe un
restore the g

It only remains to account for the third class, who had pursued their researches in the direction of Joppa, and were meditating their return to Jerusalem, when accidentally passing the mouth of a cavern they heard sounds of deep lamentation and regret. On entering the cave to ascertain the cause, they found three men answering the description of those missing, who, on being charged with the murder and finding all chance of escape cut off, made a full confession of their guilt. They were then bound and led to Jerusalem, when K S sentenced them to that death the heinousness of their crime so amply merited.

IPM *hands T B and pencil to WM.*

WM *with pencil points to various items on T B as words require* — Our M was ordered to be reinterred as near to the Sanctum Sanctorum as the Israelitish law would permit — there in a grave from the centre three feet E and three feet W, three feet between N and S, and five feet or more perpendicular. He was not buried in the Sanctum Sanctorum, because nothing

common or unclean was allowed to enter
there, not even the High Priest but once a
year, nor then until after many washings
and purifications against the great day of
expiation for sins, for by the Israelitish law,
all flesh was deemed unclean. The same
fifteen trusty FCs were ordered to attend
the funeral, clothed in white aprons and
gloves as emblems of their innocence.

You have already been informed that the
working tools with which our M was slain
were the PR, L and HM. The ornaments of
a MMs' L are the Porch, Dormer and
Square Pavement. The Porch was the
entrance to the Sanctum Sanctorum, the
Dormer the window that gave light to the
same, and the Square Pavement for the
High Priest to walk on. The High Priest's
office was to burn incense to the honour
and glory of the Most High, and to pray
fervently that the Almighty, of His un-
bounded wisdom and goodness, would be
pleased to bestow peace and tranquillity on
the Israelitish nation during the ensuing
year. The c, s, and c b, being emblems of
mortality, allude to the untimely death of

our Master HA. He was slain three
thousand years after the creation of the
world — *returns T B and pencil to IPM.*

WM — In the course of the ceremony
you have been informed of three Sns in this
Degree. The whole of them are f
corresponding in number with the f p o f.
They are the Sn of H, the Sn of S, the P Sn,
the Sn of G and D, and the Sn of J and
Exult...n, likewise called the G or R S. For
the sake of regularity I will go through them
and you will copy me — *rises with Sp.*

SD *instructs Can in whisper to take Sp
and copy Sns. He ensures Can copies Sns
correctly at appropriate places and that the
words are not repeated.*

WM *illustrates Sns as he repeats
appropriate words* — This is the Sn of H;
this, of S; this, the P Sn. The Sn of G and D
is given by passing the r h ac t f and d i o t l
e i t f o a s. This took its rise at the time our
M was making his way from the N to the E
entrance of the Temple, when his agony
was so great that the perspiration stood in
large drops on his f, and he made use of this
Sn — *illustrates, Can copies* — as a

temporary relief to his sufferings. This is the Sn of J and E. It took its rise at the time the Temple was completed, and K S with the princes of his household went to view it, when they were so struck with its magnificence that with one simultaneous motion they exclaimed — *illustrates, Can copies* — 'Oh Wonderful Masons!'

On the Continent of Europe the Sn of G and D is given in a different manner, by clasping the hs and elevating t w tr bs t t f — *illustrates, Can copies* — exclaiming 'Come — *cuts Sn, Can copies* — to my assis y c o t w' on the supposition that all MMs are bs to H A, who was a w s. In Scotland, Ireland and the States of America the Sn of G and D is given in a still different manner, by throwing u t hs with the ps extd towards the hs and d them with three distinct ms to the ss — *illustrates, Can copies* — exclaiming, O L my G, O L my G, O L my G, is there no help for the w s?

WM *sits.*

IPM *places w ts in readiness on WM's ped if he has not previously done so.*

WM — I now present to you the w ts of

a MM. They are the Sk, P, and Cs. The Sk is an implement which acts on a centre pin, whence a line is drawn to mark out ground for the foundation of the intended structure. With the P the skilful artist delineates the building in a draft or plan for the instruction and guidance of the workmen. The Cs enable him with accuracy and precision to ascertain and determine the limits and proportions of its several parts. But as we are not all operative Masons but rather free and accepted, or speculative, we apply these ts to our morals. In this sense, the Sk points out that straight and undeviating line of conduct laid down for our pursuit in the VSL; the P teaches us that our words and actions are observed and recorded by the Almighty Architect, to Whom we must give an account of our conduct through life; the Cs remind us of His unerring and impartial justice, Who, having defined for our instruction the limits of good and evil, will reward or punish as we have obeyed or disregarded His Divine commands. Thus the w ts of a MM teach us to bear in mind, and act according to, the laws of our Divine Creator, that, when we shall be summoned from this sublunary abode, we may ascend to the G L above, where the world's Great Architect lives and reigns for ever.

SD *conducts Can to seat in Lodge.*

CEREMONY
OF INSTALLATION

Note. The Ceremony is conducted from the WM's Chair by an Installed Master who will normally be the outgoing WM of the Lodge; for the sake of convenience this Installing Master is referred to as **IM**. *In the demonstrations of the Emulation Lodge of Improvement* **IM** *does work which is usually done in a regular Lodge by the DC; this is indicated by the addition of (or* **DC**).

*The Lodge is open in the First Degree.

IM *requests EAs to withdraw.*

IG *goes to door and opens it and EAs withdraw without saluting. IG closes and locks door and returns to seat.*

IM *requests two Installed Masters to occupy the chairs of SW and JW and another to act as IG.*

(**DC** *would in many Lodges conduct the various Brethren to and from their seats.*)

IM *conducts Opening the Lodge in the Second Degree or Resumes in that Degree*

*See Notes on Ritual and Procedure.

(whichever is appropriate).

A **PM goes to **ME** and conducts him by r h to a point about six or seven paces in front of WM's ped, both facing E.*

PM *Sp and Sn of F, raises ME's r h with his l h* — WM, I present to you Bro.... ......, ME of this Lodge, to receive at your hands the benefit of Installation.

IM *names PM* — Brother PM ....., your presentation shall be attended to, for which purpose I will first address a few observations to the Brethren and will then call the attention of the ME to the necessary qualifications in every candidate for the Master's chair.

PM *cuts Sn, replaces ME's r h at his side, ensures ME is on centre line of Lodge facing IM, leaves ME, and returns to his seat.*

IM — Brethren, from time immemorial it has been an established custom among Freemasons for each Lodge, once in every year at a stated period, to select from amongst those who are past Ws an experienced Craftsman to preside over

*See Notes on Ritual and Procedure.

them in the capacity of M. He must have
been regularly elected by the M, Ws, and
Brethren in open Lodge assembled, and
presented to a Board of I Ms that he may
receive from his predecessor the benefit of
installation. the better to qualify him for the
discharge of the duties of his important
trust.

Bro............ — *names ME* — you
having been so elected and presented, I
claim your attention while I recite to you
the various qualifications which are
essential in every Can for the M's Chair.
First; every Can for the office of M ought
to be of good report, true and trusty, and
held in high estimation among his Brethren
and Fs. Secondly; he must have been
regularly initiated, passed, and raised in the
established degrees of the Order, be well
skilled in the noble science. and have duly
served the office of W in a regular Lodge.
Thirdly; he ought to be exemplary in
conduct, courteous in manners, easy of
address and steady and firm in principle,
able and willing to undertake the
management of the work and well skilled in

the Ancient Charges, Regulations, and Landmarks of the Order. Can you, my worthy Brother, undertake the Mastership of·this Lodge on these qualifications?

ME — I can.

IM — Then I shall direct your attention to the Secretary while he reads to you those Ancient Charges and Regulations, to all of which your unqualified assent is essential, which you will signify by the Sn of F after each clause.

ME *faces Sec. He takes Sp after first Charge, gives and drops Sn of F. He holds Sp throughout remaining Charges and gives and drops Sn of F after each.*

Sec *stands, reads Ancient Charges from B of C, pausing after each for ME to give Sn and sits after last Charge.*

ME *faces IM.*

IM — Do you submit to, and promise to support, these Ancient Charges and Regulations as Masters have done in all ages?

ME — I do.

IM — Then you will advance to the ped and take a SO as regards your duties as M of this Lodge.

ME *advances to ped, removing glove if worn.*

IM — Kneel on your r k, place your r h on the VSL.

ME *does so.*

IM *one* ➖▮ **SW** *one* ➖▮ **JW** *one* ➖▮ .

ALL *rise, Sp and Sn of F.*

IM — Repeat your name at length, and say after me:

I, ..., in the presence of the Grand Geometrician of the Universe and of this worthy and worshipful Lodge of FC FMs, regularly held, assembled, and properly dedicated, do agree to accept the office of M of this Lodge and the duties thereof, faithfully, zealously, and impartially to administer, to the best of my skill and ability, until the next regular period of election within this Lodge, and until a successor shall have been duly elected and installed in my stead. I further solemnly promise that I will not, either during my Mastership, or at any time that the Lodge may be under my direction, permit or suffer

any deviation from the established
Landmarks of the Order: that I will not
administer, or cause to be administered,
any rite or ceremony contrary to or
subversive of our ancient Institution, but,
on the contrary, will maintain, support, and
uphold, pure and unsullied, the principles
and tenets of the Craft; that I will, to the
utmost of my power, strictly enforce
obedience to those excellent Rules and
Regulations to which I have already given
my assent, and in every respect, conscientiously discharge my duties as a ruler
in the Craft and M of this Lodge. So help
me, AG, and keep me steadfast in this my
SO of ME.

ALL *cut Sn.*

IM — As a pledge of your fidelity and to
render this a solemn Obl you will seal it
with your lips t on the VSL.

ME *does so.*

IM *takes ME's r h with his r h and raises
him* — Rise, newly obligated ME.

IM *sits.*

ALL, *except ME, sit.*

Note. If the Lodge is to be opened in

Third Degree DC will normally conduct ME to a convenient seat in the Lodge, but if it is to be resumed ME will remain standing in front of the pedestal.

IM *requests FCs to withdraw.*

IG *goes to door and opens it and FCs withdraw without saluting. IG closes and locks door and returns to seat.*

IM *conducts Opening the Lodge in the Third Degree or Resumes in that Degree (whichever is appropriate).*

IM *requests all under the rank of Installed Master to withdraw.*

IG *goes to door and opens it and MMs withdraw without saluting. IG closes and locks door and returns to seat.*

Here follows the Inner Working of the Board of Installed Masters during which the ME is installed in the Chair as WM.

Note. The WM, IM or DC should ensure that the ME understands prior to his installation that he will be required to invest the IPM during the Inner Working in the following form:

WM *rises* — Bro..........., I have much pleasure in investing you with this Jewel — *places collar on him* — as the Immediate PM of the Lodge, feeling assured from the manner in which you have transacted the business of the Lodge during your Mastership, that, should I at any time require assistance, my reliance on your co-operation will not be misplaced — *shakes hands with IPM and sits.*

The Inner Working concludes with:

IM *standing at S of WM's ped* — Bro IG, admit MMs.

*IM *(or* **DC***) goes to NE corner of Lodge and stands facing S.*

IG *goes to door, opens it, admits MMs, closes and locks door and returns to seat.*

MMs enter without saluting and form a line along N side of Lodge facing S so that IM (or DC) is at E end of the line.

IM — Brethren, you will pass round the Lodge and salute the WM as MMs.

IM *(or* **DC***), followed by MMs, turns l and proceeds round Lodge 'squaring' each corner. During this permabulation each stops with r h in h of l f in front of WM's ped and (still facing S) gives and cuts MM P Sn including recovery and continues till reaching former position in N, faces S making a line as before.*

IM *at S of WM's ped* — Brethren, during your temporary absence Brother ...... has been regularly installed in the Chair of KS according to ancient custom, and I

*See Notes on Ritual and Procedure.

now for the first time proclaim him WM of the ...... Lodge, No ...... in the Register of the Grand Lodge of England, until the next regular period of election within this Lodge and until a successor shall have been duly elected and installed in his stead, and I call on you to greet him as MMs with t, taking the time from me (*or — from the DC — if the time is to be taken from him*).

IM (*or **DC** going to a convenient point facing the line of MMs*) — To order, Brethren — *Sp, then G or R Sn t times, the meeting of the hands together and with the sides being made audibly.**

MMs *take Sp when IM (or DC) does and give G or R Sn audibly in unison with IM (or DC).*

(*If **DC** has given time, he returns to E end of line of MMs*)

IPM *places w ts of MM in readiness on WM's ped if he has not already done so.*

IM *at S of WM's ped, to WM.* I now present to you the w ts of a MM — *and continues with the full explanation.**

IM *to WM* — You will now close the

*See Notes on Ritual and Procedure.

Lodge in the Third Degree — *sits*.

WM *conducts Closing the Lodge in the Third Degree, after which —*

*IM *stands* — Bro IG, admit FCs *(if leading perambulations, goes to E end of line of MMs)*.

IG *goes to door, opens it, admits any FCs, closes and locks door and returns to seat.*

Any FCs enter without saluting and join line of MMs in N, standing immediately on r of IM (or DC) and face S.

IM — Brethren, you will pass round the Lodge and salute the WM as FCs.

IM *(or DC), followed by FCs and MMs, turns l and proceeds round Lodge 'squaring' each corner. During this perambulation each stops with r h in h of l f in front of WM's ped, and (still facing S) gives and cuts FC Sn and continues till reaching former position in N, faces S making a line as before.*

IM *(if not leading perambulation, joins the line after last MM has saluted) proceeds with line only as far as N of SW's*

**See Notes on Ritual and Procedure.*

ped where he halts and faces E.

IM *waits at N of SW's ped till line is reformed in N —* Brethren, during your temporary absence Brother ...... has been regularly installed in the Chair of K S according to ancient custom and I now for the second time proclaim him WM of the ...... Lodge, No ...... in the Register of the Grand Lodge of England, until the next regular period of election within this Lodge, and until a successor shall have been duly elected and installed in his stead and I call on you to greet him as FCs with f, taking the time from me *(or — from the DC — if the time is to be taken from him).*

IM *(or* **DC** *going to a convenient point facing the line of Brethren) —* To order, Brethren — Sp and FC Sn which he holds — b, h bdge. — *He then gives b, h bdge f times, each impact of the r h being made audibly.*

MMs *and* **FCs** *take Sp and give FC Sn and hold it when IM (or DC) does and give b, h bdge greeting f times audibly in unison with IM (or DC).*

IM *returns to E, at S of WM's ped.*

(If DC has given time, he returns to E end of line of Brethren).

IPM *places w ts of FC, in readiness on WM's ped if he has not already done so.*

IM *to WM* — I now present to you the w ts of a FC FM — *and continues with the full explanation.**

IM *to WM* — You will now close the Lodge in the Second Degree — *sits.*

WM *conducts Closing the Lodge in the Second Degree, after which —*

IM *stands* — Bro IG, admit EAs *(if leading perambulations, goes to E end of line of Brethren).*

IG *goes to door, opens it, admits any EAs, closes and locks door and returns to seat.*

Any EAs enter without saluting and join line of Brethren in N, standing immediately on r of IM (or DC) and face S.

IM — Brethren, you will pass round the Lodge and salute the WM as EAs.

IM *(or* **DC***) and EAs, FCs and MMs following him turn l and proceed round Lodge 'squaring' each corner. During this*

See Notes on Ritual and Procedure.

*perambulation each stops with r h in h of l f
in front of WM's ped, still facing S, gives
and cuts EA Sn and continues till reaching
former position in N, faces S making a line
as before.*

IM *(if not leading perambulation, joins
the line after last MM has saluted)
proceeds with line only as far as W of JW's
ped where he halts and faces N.*

IM *waits at W of JW's ped, till line is
reformed in N* — Brethren, during your
temporary absence Brother ...... has been
regularly installed in the Chair of K S
according to ancient custom and I now for
the third time proclaim him WM of the ......
Lodge, No ...... in the Register of the
Grand Lodge of England, until the next
regular period of election within this Lodge,
and until a successor shall have been duly
elected and installed in his stead, and I call
on you to greet him as EAs with t taking
the time from me *(or — from the DC — if
the time is to be taken from him).*

IM *(or **DC** going to a convenient point
facing the line of Brethren)* — To order,
Brethren — *Sp and EA Sn t times, the final*

movement of the r h for each Sn making an audible impact on the thigh.

MMs, FCs and EAs take Sp when IM (or DC) does and give EA Sn t times audibly in unison with IM (or DC).

IM *returns to E, at S of WM's ped (If* **DC** *has given time, he returns to E end of line of Brethren.)*

IPM *places w ts of EA in readiness on WM's ped if he has not already done so.*

IM *to WM* — I now present to you the w ts of an EA FM — *and continues with the full explanation.**

IM *to line of Brethren* — Be seated, Brethren.

DC *and Brethren resume their seats.*

IPM *hands Lodge Warrant to IM.*

***IM** *opens Warrant, and hands it to* WM — WM, I now deliver into your special keeping the Warrant of the Lodge. It has been for many years entrusted to the hands of very worthy and distinguished Brethren, and I am sure that in delivering it into your charge it will lose none of its former splendour, but will be transmitted to

See Notes on Ritual and Procedure.

your successor pure and unsullied as you now receive it.

IPM *hands B of C and By-laws to IM.*

IM *to WM* — The B of C I also present to you — *hands B of C to WM* which I strongly recommend to your notice, for you will find that there is scarcely a case of difficulty can occur in the Lodge in which that book will not set you right. These — *hands By-laws to WM* — are the By-laws of your Lodge (which I recommend you to have read at least once in the year in order that the Brethren may not plead ignorance of them).†

IM *to WM* — You will now appoint and invest your officers.

Note. The presentation of officers for investiture may be done either by **IM** *or* **DC**. *Whichever is to do this now goes to a point facing the WM's ped and a convenient distance from it. If the DC is to carry out the duty, IM sits.*

Note. All officers to be invested who are

---

†*Grand Lodge (12 September 1979) suggested that the recommendation contained in the words in brackets 'should be excised from the ceremonial.'*

*PMs are taken to S of WM's ped, other Brn
to N side, in each case facing WM* **IM** *(or*
DC) *hands Collar etc to WM at
appropriate time for each investiture.*

IM *(or* **DC**) *facing WM's ped, Sp and
EA Sn* — WM, whom do you appoint your
SW?

WM — Bro .... *(named Brother
rises).*

IM *(or* **DC**) *cuts Sn, collects appropriate
Collar, Gavel and Cn. and conducts named
Bro by the r h to WM's ped.*

WM *rises* — *to new SW* — Bro ....,
I appoint you my SW, and I now invest you
with the insignia of your office — *invests
SW with Collar* — The L — *takes it in l h*
— being an emblem of equality, points out
the equal measures you are bound to
pursue in conjunction with me in the well
ruling and governing of the Lodge —
releases L — I therefore place in your hand
this Gavel — *hands Gavel* — as an
emblem of power, to enable you to assist
me in preserving order in the Lodge,
especially in the W. I also present to you
the Cn of your office — *hands Cn* —

which you will place erect when the Lodge
is opened to point out to the Brethren that
the Lodge is engaged in Masonic business.
Your place is in the W, your duty to mark
the setting sun, to close the Lodge by my
command, after having seen that every
Brother has had his due — *shakes hands
with SW and sits.*

IM *(or* **DC***) conducts SW to l side of
chair at SW's ped direct.*

SW *places Gavel and Cn in position and
sits.*

IM *(or* **DC***) conducts PM who has acted
as SW to a seat.*

IM *(or* **DC***) goes to point facing WM's
ped, Sp and EA Sn* — WM, whom do you
appoint your JW?

WM — Bro .... *(named Bro rises).*

IM *(or* **DC***) cuts Sn, collects appropriate
Collar, Gavel and Cn and conducts named
Brother by the r h to appropriate side of
WM's ped.*

WM *rises* — Bro ...., I appoint you
my JW, and I now invest you with the
Collar and Jewel of your office — *invests
JW with Collar* — The P R — *takes it in l*

h — being an emblem of uprightness, points out the integrity of the measures you are bound to pursue in conjunction with me and your Brother SW in the well ruling and governing of the Lodge — *releases P R* — particularly in the examination of Visitors, lest through your neglect any unqualified person should gain admission to our assemblies and the Brethren be thereby innocently led to violate their Obl. I therefore place in your hand this Gavel — *hands Gavel* — as an emblem of power to enable you to assist me and your Brother SW in preserving order in the Lodge, especially in the S. I also present to you the Cn of your office — *hands Cn* — which you will place horizontal whenever the Lodge is opened for business and erect whenever the Lodge is called from labour to refreshment, that matter being under your immediate supervision as the ostensible steward of the Lodge. Your place is in the S, your duty to mark the sun at its meridian, to call the Brethren from labour to refreshment and from refreshment to labour, that profit and pleasure may be the result — *shakes hands with JW and sits.*

IM *(or* **DC***) conducts JW to l side of chair at JW's ped direct.*

JW *places Gavel and Cn in position and sits.*

IM *(or* **DC***) conducts PM who has acted as JW to a seat.*

**If a Chaplain is to be appointed —*

IM *(or* **DC***) goes to point facing WM's ped, Sp and EA Sn —* WM, whom do you appoint Chaplain?

WM — Bro .... *(named Bro rises).*

IM *(or* **DC** *cuts sign, collects appropriate Collar and conducts named Bro by the r h to appropriate side of WM's ped.*

WM *rises, invests Chaplain with suitable words, shakes hands with him when the investiture is finished and sits.*

IM *(or* **DC***) conducts Chaplain to his seat.]*

IM *(or* **DC***) goes to point facing WM's ped, Sp and EA Sn —* WM, Bro .... having been elected Treasurer of the Lodge,

**See Notes on Ritual and Procedure.*

will you please invest him? *(or other suitable words)*.

WM — I will *(or other appropriate words) and named Bro rises.*

IM *(or* **DC***) cuts Sn, collects appropriate Collar and conducts Treasurer elect by the r h to appropriate side of WM's ped.*

WM *rises* — Bro ...., you having been elected Treasurer of the Lodge, I now invest you with the insignia of your office — *invests Treasurer with Collar and takes Jewel in l h* — which is a key appended to a collar — *releases Jewel, shakes hands with Treasurer and sits.*

IM *(or* **DC***) conducts Treasurer to his seat.*

IM *(or* **DC***) goes to point facing WM's ped, Sp and EA Sn* — WM, whom do you appoint Secretary?

WM — Bro .... *(named Bro rises).*

IM *(or* **DC***) cuts Sn, collects appropriate Collar and conducts named Bro by the r h to appropriate side of WM's ped.*

WM *rises* — Bro ...., I appoint you Secretary of the Lodge and I now invest you with the jewel of your office — *invests*

Secretary with Collar and takes jewel in l h — which is two pens in saltire — releases jewel, shakes hands with Secretary and sits.

IM (*or* **DC**) *conducts Secretary to his seat.*

IM (*or* **DC**) *goes to point facing WM's ped, Sp and EA Sn* — WM, whom do you appoint DC?

WM — Bro .... (*named Bro rises*).

IM (*or* **DC**) *cuts Sn, collects appropriate Collar and Wand and conducts named Bro by the r h to appropriate side of WM's ped.*

WM *rises, invests DC with suitable words, shakes hands with him when the investiture is finished and sits.*

IM (*or* **DC**) *conducts DC to his seat and in the case of a PM or a DC not reappointed takes a seat in the Lodge.*

IM (*or* **DC**) *goes to point facing WM's ped, Sp and EA Sn* — WM, whom do you appoint SD?

WM — Bro .... (*named Bro rises*).

IM (*or* **DC**) *collects appropriate Collar and Wand and conducts named Bro by the r h to appropriate side of WM's ped.*

WM *rises* — Bro ...., I appoint you
SD of the Lodge and I now invest you with
the jewel of your office — *invests SD with
Collar and takes Jewel in l h* — which is a
dove bearing an olive branch — *releases
Jewel* — Your place is at or near to my
right, your duty to bear all messages and
commands from me to the SW and await
the return of the JD. It is also part of your
duty to attend on Candidates during the
Ceremonies of Passing and Raising. I
therefore entrust you with this wand as a
badge of your office — *hands wand to
SD's r h* — not doubting you will exercise
the care and attention that office requires
— *shakes hands with SD and sits.*

IM *(or DC) conducts SD to his seat.*

IM *(or DC) goes to point facing WM's
ped, Sp and EA Sn* — WM, whom do you
appoint JD?

WM— Bro .... *(named Bro rises).*

IM *(or DC) cuts Sn, collects appropriate
Collar and Wand and conducts named
Bro by the r h to appropriate side of
WM's ped.*

WM *rises* — Bro ...., I appoint you

JD of the Lodge and I now invest you with the jewel of your office — *invests JD with Collar and takes Jewel in l h* — which is similar in every respect to that of the SD — *releases Jewel* — Your place is at the right of the SW, your duty to carry all my messages and communications from the S to the JW and to see that the same are punctually obeyed. It is also part of your duty to attend on Candidates during the Ceremony of Initiation and to assist the SD while attending on Candidates during the Ceremonies of Passing and Raising. I therefore place in your hand this wand — *hands wand to JD's r h* — as a badge of your office, which I have no doubt you will fill with proper care and attention — *shakes hands with JD and sits.*

IM *(or* **DC***) conducts JD to his seat.*

*(In Lodges where a Charity Steward, an Almoner, ADC or Organist is appointed, they are invested in that order and by the same procedure.

IM *(or* **DC***) goes to point facing WM's ped, Sp and EA Sn* — WM, whom do you appoint . . . ?

* See Notes on Ritual and Procedure.

WM — Bro .... *(named Bro rises).*

IM *(or* **DC***) cuts Sn, collects appropriate Collar and conducts named Bro by the r h to appropriate side of WM's ped.*

WM *rises and invests the Officer with appropriate words, shakes hands with him and sits.*

IM *(or* **DC***) conducts the Officer to his seat in the Lodge.)*

IM *(or* **DC***) goes to point facing WM's ped, Sp and EA Sn —* WM, whom do you appoint Assistant Secretary?

WM — Bro .... *(named Bro rises).*

IM *(or* **DC***) cuts Sn, collects appropriate Collar and conducts named Bro by the r h to appropriate side of WM's ped.*

WM *rises —* Bro ...., I appoint you Assistant Secretary of the Lodge and I now invest you with the jewel of your office — *invests Assistant Secretary with Collar and takes Jewel in l h —* which is two pens in saltire — *releases Jewel, shakes hands with Assistant Secretary and sits.*

IM *(or* **DC***) conducts Assistant Secretary to his seat.*

IM *(or* **DC***) goes to point facing WM's*

H

ped, Sp and EA Sn — WM, whom do you appoint IG?

WM — Bro .... *(named Bro rises).*

IM *(or* **DC***) cuts Sn, collects appropriate Collar and conducts named Bro by the r h to appropriate side of WM's ped.*

WM *rises* — Bro ...., I appoint you IG of the Lodge and I now invest you with the jewel of your office — *invests IG with Collar and takes insignia in l h* — which is two swords in saltire. — *releases* — Your place is within the entrance of the Lodge, your duty to report to the Master when Brethren claim admission, to admit Masons on proof, receive the Candidates in due form and obey the commands of the JW — *shakes hands with IG and sits.*

IM *(or* **DC***) conducts IG to his seat and then conducts PM who has acted as IG to a seat.*

(*If Stewards are to be appointed **IM** *(or* **DC***) goes to point facing WM's ped, Sp and EA Sn* — WM, whom do you appoint Stewards?

WM — Brothers ......, ..., etc *(named* **See Notes on Ritual and Procedure.*

Brethren rise).

IM *(or* **DC***) collects appropriate Collars and conducts named Brethren to appropriate side of WM's ped.*

WM *rises and invests each Steward with appropriate words according to the custom of the Lodge, shakes each by the hand, and, when all have been invested, sits.*

IM *(or* **DC***) conducts the Stewards to their seats.)*

IM *(or* **DC***) takes a seat.*

WM — *double* ➡✦.

IG *goes to door, admits Tyler, closes and locks door, and returns to his seat.*

Tyler, *holding Swd in l h, pt down, and carrying Collar, goes to N of SW's ped, Sp and EA Sn. He then walks direct to appropriate side of WM's ped, hands Collar to WM and places Swd diagonally across VSL.*

*Note. In E L of I Tyler is not conducted to and from WM's ped and Tyler places Swd diagonally across VSL. In many Lodges **DC** *conducts Tyler, after he has saluted, to WM's ped and after investiture,*

*See Notes on Ritual and Procedure.

back to N of SW's ped. Also, many Lodges prefer the procedure whereby the Swd is placed on the ped and not on VSL.

WM *rises and takes collar* — Bro ...., you having been elected Tyler of the Lodge, I now invest you with the jewel of your office — *invests Tyler with Collar and takes Jewel in l h* — which is a sword appended to a Collar. — *releases Jewel* — Your place is outside the door of the Lodge, your duty, to see that the Candidates are properly prepared and to give the proper reports on the door of the Lodge when Candidates, members, or visitors require admission. I therefore place in your hand this sword — *hands sword, point down, to Tyler who takes it with his r h and transfers it to his l h* — to enable you to keep off all intruders and cowans to Masonry, and suffer none to pass but such as are duly qualified. From you well known zeal, I am sure that the confidence which the Brethren have shown by your election will not be misplaced — *shakes hands with Tyler and sits.*

Tyler *proceeds direct to N of SW's ped,*

faces WM, Sp, EA Sn and retires from Lodge.

IG *goes to door in front of Tyler, opens it and, when Tyler has gone out, closes and locks door and returns to seat.*

*Note. In EL of I the three addresses following are all delivered by IM.

ADDRESS TO THE WM

IM *(or other* **PM***) goes direct to N of SW's ped and faces WM* — WM, you, having been installed in the Chair of this worthy and worshipful Lodge, cannot be insensible to the obligations which devolve on you as its head, or to your responsibility for the faithful discharge of the duties annexed to the appointment. The honour, reputation, and usefulness of this Lodge will materially depend on the skill and assiduity with which you manage its concerns; while the happiness of its members will be generally promoted in proportion to the zeal and ability with which you promulgate the genuine principles of the Institution. As a pattern for imitation, consider that

*See Notes on Ritual and Procedure.

glorious luminary of Nature, which, rising in the E, regularly diffuses light and lustre to all within its circle; in like manner it is your peculiar province to communicate light and instruction to the Brethren of your Lodge. Forcibly impress upon them the dignity and high importance of Masonry; seriously admonish them never to disgrace it; charge them to practise out of the Lodge those duties they have been taught in it; and by virtuous, amiable, and discreet conduct to prove to the world the happy and beneficial effects of our Ancient Institution, so that when anyone is said to be a member of it, the world may know that he is one to whom the burdened heart may pour forth its sorrow, to whom the distressed may prefer their suit, whose hand is guided by justice, and whose heart is expanded by benevolence. In fine, WM, by a strict observance of the By-laws of your Lodge, the Constitutions of Masonry, and above all by the use of the Sacred Writings which are given as the rule and guide of our Faith, you will be enabled to lay up a Crown of Joy and Rejoicing which will continue when time with you shall be no more — *Sn of R*. And may God grant you health and strength to perform the duties of your high office with satisfaction to yourself, and advantage to your Lodge — *drops Sn of R and return to E, S of WM's ped (or, for a PM, resumes his seat).*

ADDRESS TO THE WARDENS

IM *(or other* **PM),** *from S of WM's ped, facing W* — Brother S and JWs, the WM having appointed you to the principal offices, you are to consider yourselves pledged by your acceptance thereof to a strict performance of your duties, as well as to a regular attendance during the time for which you are appointed. You are sufficiently acquainted with the principles of Masonry to prevent any mistrust that you will be found wanting in the discharge of the duties of your respective offices. Suffice it to say that what you observe praiseworthy in others you should carefully imitate, and what in them may appear defective you should in yourselves amend. You ought to be examples of good order and regularity, for it is only by paying due obedience to the laws in our own conduct that we can reasonably expect compliance with them from others. You are assiduously to assist the WM in the discharge of the duties of his important trust, by communicating L and imparting knowledge to all whom he may place under your direction. From the spirit you have hitherto evinced, we entertain no doubt your future conduct will be such as to merit the esteem of your Brethren and the gratifying testimony of a clear conscience.

ADDRESS TO THE BRETHREN

IM (*or other* **PM**) *from S of WM's ped, facing W* — Brethren, such is the nature of our Constitution that as some must of necessity rule and teach, so others must of course learn, submit, and obey. Humility in each is an essential qualification. The Brethren whom the WM has selected to assist him in the ruling and governing of the Lodge are too well acquainted with the principles of Masonry, and the Laws of our Institution, to warrant any mistrust that

they will be found wanting in the discharge
of the duties of their respective offices, or
that they will exceed the powers with which
they are entrusted; and you, Brethren, I am
sure, are of too generous a disposition to
envy their preferment. I therefore trust that
we shall have but one aim in view, to please
each other and unite in the grand design of
being happy and communicating happiness.
And as this association has been formed
and perfected with so much unanimity and
concord, long may it continue. May
brotherly love and affection ever distinguish
us as men and as Masons. May the
principles and tenets of our profession,
which are founded on the basis of religious
truth and virtue, teach us to measure our
actions by the rule of rectitude, square our
conduct by the principles of morality, and
guide our inclinations, and even our
thoughts, within the compass of propriety.
Hence we learn to be meek, humble and
resigned; to be faithful to our God, our
Country, and our Laws; to drop a tear of
sympathy over the failings of a Brother;
and to pour the healing balm of consolation

into the bosom of the afflicted. May these principles and tenets be transmitted pure and unpolluted, through this Lodge from generation to generation.

APPENDIX

The matter contained
in this Appendix is
NOT EMULATION WORKING
(see Preface)

CONTENTS OF APPENDIX

HYMNS WHICH MAY BE SUNG

AT THE
OPENING OF THE LODGE

Hail Eternal! by whose aid
   All created things were made;
Heav'n and earth, Thy vast design;
   Hear us, Architect Divine!

May our work, begun in Thee,
   Ever blest with order be,
And may we, when labours cease
   Part in harmony and peace.

By Thy glorious Majesty —
   By the trust we place in Thee —
By the badge and mystic sign —
   Hear us, Architect Divine!
     SO MOTE IT BE.

AT THE
CLOSING OF THE LODGE

Now the evening shadows closing,
    Warn from toil to peaceful rest,
Mystic arts and rights reposing,
    Sacred in each faithful breast.

God of Light! whose love unceasing,
    Doth to all Thy works extend,
Crown our Order with Thy blessing,
    Build; sustain us to the end.

Humbly now we bow before Thee
    Grateful for Thy aid Divine;
Everlasting power and glory,
    Mighty Architect! be Thine.
        SO MOTE IT BE.

AN EXPLANATION OF THE FIRST DEGREE TRACING BOARD

The practice of including the explanation of the Tracing Board of the First Degree as an essential part of that Ceremony has fallen into disuse. The explanation was intended to be capable of being divided up so as also to form part of the First Lecture and may be found in Sections 3, 4, 5, 6 and 7 of that Lecture. The explanation is still, however, sometimes given as a separate explanation as below, with the introductory paragraph customarily used, which is from Preston's *Illustrations of Masonry*.

The usages and customs among Freemasons have ever borne a near affinity to those of the ancient Egyptians. Their philosophers, unwilling to expose their mysteries to vulgar eyes, couched their systems of learning and polity under signs and hieroglyphical figures, which were communicated to their chief priests or Magi alone, who were bound by solemn oath to conceal them. The system of Pythagoras was founded on a similar principle, as well as many others of more recent date. Masonry, however, is not only the most ancient but the most honourable society that ever existed, as there is not a character or emblem here depicted but serves to inculcate the principles of piety and virtue among all its genuine professors.

Let me first call your attention to the form of the Lodge which is a parallel-epipedon, in length from E to W, in breadth between N and S, in depth from the surface of the earth to the centre, and even as high as the heavens. The reason a Freemasons' Lodge is described in this vast extent is to show the universality of the science; likewise, a Mason's charity should know no bounds save those of prudence.

Our Lodges stand on holy ground, because the first Lodge was consecrated on account of three grand offerings thereon made, which met with Divine approbation. First, the ready compliance of Abraham with the will of God in not refusing to offer up his son Isaac as a burnt sacrifice, when it pleased the Almighty to substitute a more agreeable victim in his stead. Secondly, the

many pious prayers and ejaculations of
King David, which actually appeased the
wrath of God, and stayed a pestilence
which then raged among his people, owing
to his inadvertently having them numbered.
Thirdly, the many thanksgivings, oblations,
burnt sacrifices, and costly offerings, which
Solomon, King of Israel, made at the
completion, dedication and consecration of
the Temple at Jerusalem to God's service.
Those three did then, do now, and I trust
ever will, render the ground of Freemasonry holy.

Our Lodges are situated due E and W
because all places of Divine worship, as
well as Mason's regular, well-formed,
constituted Lodges, are, or ought to be, so
situated: for which we assign three Masonic
reasons: first, the Sun, the Glory of the
Lord, rises in the E and sets in the W;
second, learning originated in the E, and
thence spread its benign influence to the W;
the third, last, and grand reason,* which is
too long to be entered upon now, is
explained in the course of our Lectures,

*See Fourth Section of First Lecture.

which I hope you will have many
opportunities of hearing.

Our Lodges are supported by three great
pillars. They are called Wisdom, Strength,
and Beauty: Wisdom to contrive, Strength
to support, and Beauty to adorn; Wisdom
to conduct us in all our undertakings,
Strength to support us under all our
difficulties, and Beauty to adorn the inward
man. The Universe is the Temple of the
Deity whom we serve; Wisdom, Strength,
and Beauty are about His throne as pillars
of His works, for His Wisdom is infinite,
His Strength omnipotent, and Beauty
shines through the whole of the creation in
symmetry and order. The Heavens He has
stretched forth as a canopy; the earth He
has planted as a footstool; He crowns His
Temple with Stars as with a diadem, and
with His hand He extends the Power and
Glory. The Sun and Moon are messengers
of His will, and all His Law is concord. The
three great pillars supporting a FMs' Lodge
are emblematic of those Divine attributes,
and further represent S K of I, H K of T,
and H A; S K or I for His Wisdom in

building, completing and dedicating the
Temple of Jerusalem to God's service; H K
of T for his Strength in supporting him with
men and materials: and H A for his curious
and masterly workmanship in beautifying
and adorning the same. But as we have no
noble orders of Architecture known by the
names of Wisdom, Strength, and Beauty,
we refer them to the three most celebrated,
which are the Ionic, Doric and Corinthian.

The covering of a Freemasons' Lodge is
a celestial canopy of divers colours even the
Heavens. The way by which we, as
Masons, hope to arrive there is by the
assistance of a ladder, in Scripture called
Jacob's ladder. It is composed of many
staves or rounds, which point out as many
moral virtues, but three principal ones,
which are Faith, Hope and Charity: Faith
in the Great Architect of the Universe,
Hope in salvation, and to be in Charity with
all men. It reaches to the Heavens, and
rests on the VSL, because, by the doctrines
contained in that Holy Book, we are taught
to believe in the dispensations of Divine
Providence, which belief strengthens our

Faith, and enables us to ascend the first step; this Faith naturally creates in us a Hope of becoming partakers of the blessed promises therein recorded, which Hope enables us to ascend the second step; but the third and last, being Charity, comprehends the whole, and the Mason who is possessed of this virtue in its most ample sense may justly be deemed to have attained the summit of his profession; figuratively speaking, an Ethereal Mansion veiled from mortal eyes by the starry firmament, emblematically depicted here by seven stars, which have an allusion to as many regularly made Masons, without which number no Lodge is perfect, neither can any candidate be legally initiated into the Order.

The interior of a Freemason's Lodge is composed of Ornaments, Furniture, and Jewels. The Ornaments of the Lodge are the Mosaic pavement, the Blazing Star, and the Indented or Tessellated Border; the Mosaic pavement is the beautiful flooring of the Lodge, the Blazing Star the Glory in the centre, and the indented or Tessellated

Border the skirtwork round the same. The Mosaic pavement may justly be deemed the beautiful flooring of a Freemason's Lodge, by reason of its being variegated and chequered. This points out the diversity of objects which decorate and adorn the creation, the animate as well as the inanimate parts thereof. The Blazing Star, or Glory in the centre, refers us to the Sun, which enlightens the earth, and by its benign influence dispenses its blessings to mankind in general. The Indented or Tessellated Border refers us to the Planets, which in their various revolutions form a beautiful border or skirtwork round that Grand Luminary, the Sun, as the other does round that of a Freemasons' Lodge. The furniture of the Lodge consists of the VSL, the Cs and Sq; the S Ws are to rule and govern our faith, on them we O our Candidates for Freemasonry; so are the Cs and Sq when united, to regulate our lives and actions. The Sacred Volume is derived from God to man in general, the Cs belong to the Grand Master in particular, and the Sq to the whole Craft.

The Jewels of the Lodge are three movable and three immovable. The movable Jewels are the Sq, L, and P R. Among operative Masons the Sq is to try, and adjust, rectangular corners of buildings, and assist in bringing rude matter into due form: the L to lay levels and prove horizontals: the P R to try, and adjust, uprights, while fixing them on their proper bases. Among Free and Accepted Masons, the Sq teaches morality, the L equality, and the P R justness and uprightness of life and actions. They are called Movable Jewels, because they are worn by the Master and his Wardens, and are transferable to their successors on nights of Installation. The Master is distinguished by the Sq, the Senior Warden by the L, and the Junior Warden by the P R. The Immovable Jewels are the Tracing Board, the Rough and Perfect Ashlars. The Tracing Board is for the Master to lay lines and draw designs on; the Rough Ashlar for the EA to work, mark and indent on; and the Perfect Ashlar for the experienced Craftsman to try, and adjust, his jewels on. They are called

Immovable Jewels, because they lie open and immovable in the Lodge for the Brethren to moralise on.

As the Tracing Board is for the Master to lay lines and draw designs on, the better to enable the Brethren to carry on the intended structure with regularity and propriety, so the VSL may justly be deemed the Spiritual Tracing Board of the Great Architect of the Universe, in which are laid down such Divine Laws and Moral Plans, that were we conversant therein, and adherent thereto, would bring us to an Ethereal Mansion not made with hands, eternal in the Heavens. The Rough Ashlar is a stone, rough and unhewn as taken from the quarry, until by the industry and ingenuity of the workman it is modelled, wrought into due form, and rendered fit for the intended structure; this represents man in his infant or primitive state, rough and unpolished as that stone, until, by the kind care and attention of his parents or guardians, in giving him a liberal and virtuous education, his mind becomes cultivated, and he is thereby rendered a fit

member of civilised society. The Perfect
Ashlar is a stone of a true die or square, fit
only to be tried by the Sq and Cs; this
represents man in the decline of years, after
a regular well-spent life in acts of piety and
virtue, which can no otherwise be tried and
approved than by the Sq of God's Word
and the C of his own self-convincing
conscience.

In all regular, well-formed, constituted
Lodges there is a point within a circle round
which the Brethren cannot err; this circle is
bounded between North and South by two
grand parallel lines, one representing
Moses, and the other King Solomon; on the
upper part of this circle rests the VSL,
supporting Jacob's Ladder, the top of
which reaches to the Heavens; and were we
as conversant in that Holy Book, and as
adherent to the doctrines therein contained
as those parallels were, it would bring us to
Him who would not deceive us, neither will
He suffer deception. In going round this
circle, we must necessarily touch on both
those parallel lines, likewise on the S V; and
while a Mason keeps himself thus

circumscribed, he cannot err.

The word Lewis denotes strength, and is here depicted by certain pieces of metal dovetailed into a stone, forming a cramp, and when in combination with some of the mechanical powers, such as a system of pulleys, it enables the operative Mason to raise great weights to certain heights with little encumbrance, and to fix them on their proper bases. Lewis likewise denotes the son of a Mason; his duty to his aged parents is to bear the heat and burden of the day, which they, by reason of their age, ought to be exempt from; to assist them in time of need, and thereby render the close of their days happy and comfortable: his privilege for so doing is that of being made a Mason before any other person, however dignified.

Pendent to the corners of the Lodge are four tassels, meant to remind us of the four cardinal virtues, namely: Temperance, Fortitude, Prudence, and Justice, the whole of which, tradition informs us, were constantly practised by a great majority of our ancient Brethren. The distinguishing characteristics of a good Freemason are

Virtue, Honour, and Mercy, and may they ever be found in a Freemason's breast.

ADDITIONAL EXPLANATION OF THE APRON IN THE FIRST DEGREE

You will observe that this Apron is made from the skin of a Lamb, and as the Lamb had been from time immemorial the universally acknowledged emblem of purity and innocence, you will be thereby reminded of that purity of life and actions which should at all times distinguish a FM, and which is most essential to your gaining admission to that Grand Lodge Above where the blessed ever rest in eternal peace.

I trust you may live many years to wear that badge with pleasure to yourself, usefulness to the Craft, and honour to the Lodge in which you have been initiated, and let me further exhort you never to disgrace it, for you may be assured it will never disgrace you.

LONG EXPLANATION
OF THE
WORKING TOOLS OF
SECOND DEGREE

Sometimes a longer explanation of the symbolic teaching of the working tools of the Second Degree is given as follows, but it is only adopted in the 'Emulation' working in the course of the Lectures, where it applies to the three Movable Jewels. (See First Lecture, Fifth Section.)

The Sq teaches us to regulate our lives and actions according to the Masonic line and rule, and to harmonise our conduct in this life so as to render us acceptable to that Divine Being from whom all goodness springs, and to whom we must give an account of all our actions.

The L demonstrates that we are all sprung from the same stock, partakers of the same nature and sharers in the same hope; and although distinctions among men are necessary to preserve subordination, yet ought no eminence of situation make us forget that we are Brothers, for he who is placed on the lowest spoke of fortune's wheel is equally entitled to our regard, as a time will come — and the wisest of us knows not how soon — when all distinctions, save those of goodness and virtue, shall cease, and death, the grand leveller of all human greatness, reduce us to the same state.

The infallible P R, which, like Jacob's ladder, connects heaven and earth, is the criterion of rectitude and truth. It teaches us to walk justly and uprightly before God and man, neither turning to the right nor left from the paths of virtue; not to be an enthusiast, persecutor, or slanderer of religion, neither bending towards avarice, injustice, malice, revenge, nor the envy and contempt of mankind, but giving up every selfish propensity which might injure others. To steer the bark of this life over the seas of passion without quitting the helm of rectitude is the highest perfection to which human nature can attain; and as the builder raises his column by the level and perpendicular, so ought every Mason to conduct himself towards this world, to observe a due medium between avarice and profusion, to hold the scales of justice with equal poise, to make his passions and prejudices coincide with the just line of his conduct, and in all his pursuits to have eternity in view.

Thus, the Sq teaches morality, the L equality, and the P R justness and uprightness of life and actions.

CHARGE AFTER PASSING

WM *(to Can)* — Having advanced to the Second Degree, we congratulate you on your preferment. It is unnecessary to recapitulate the duties which as a Mason you are bound to discharge, or to enlarge on the necessity of a strict adherence to them, as your own experience must have established their value. Your behaviour and regular deportment have merited the honour which we have conferred; and in your new character it is expected that you will not only conform to the principles of the Order, but steadily persevere in the practice of every virtue. The study of the liberal Arts, which tends so effectually to polish and adorn the mind, is earnestly recommended to your consideration, especially the Science of Geometry, which is established as the basis of our Art. As the solemnity of our Ceremonies requires a serious deportment, you are to be particularly attentive to your behaviour in our assemblies; you are to preserve our ancient usages and customs sacred and inviolable, and induce others by your example to hold them in veneration. The laws and regulations of the Order you are strenuously to support and maintain. You are not to palliate or aggravate the offences of your Brethren; but in the decision of every trespass against our rules, judge with candour, admonish with friendship, and reprehend with mercy. As a Craftsman, in our private assemblies you may offer your opinions on such subjects as are introduced in the lecture, under the superintendence of an experienced Master, who will guard the Landmarks against encroachment. By this privilege you may improve your intellectual powers, qualify yourself to become a useful member of society, and, like a skilful Brother, strive to excel in what is good and great. You are duly to honour and obey all regular Signs and Summonses given and received. You are to encourage industry, and reward merit, supply the wants and relieve the necessities of Brethren and Fellows to the utmost of your power and ability, and on no account to wrong them, or see them wronged, but timely to apprise them of approaching danger, and to view their interests as inseparable from your own. Such is the nature of your engagements as a Fellow-Craft, and these duties you are bound by the most sacred ties to observe.

I

ADDITIONAL EXPLANATION
OF THE TRACING BOARD
OF THE SECOND DEGREE

The word .... takes its rise from the following remarkable fact. When the C of I had repeatedly forsaken the laws of their forefathers, and long persisted in their idolatrous ways, the Almighty thought proper to afflict them with divers punishments; one of the most grievous of which was subjecting them to the inroads and oppressions of neighbouring Gentile nations. When, however, the people repented of their idolatry, and humbled themselves before the true God, He never failed to raise them up a champion and deliverer. There lived in Israel a man of repute whose name was Gilead, and who had many sons; but one in particular, called Jephtha, whom he had by a concubine. Gilead dying, and his sons being grown up, they expelled Jephtha from his father's house, saying: 'Thinkest thou, who art but the son of a bond-woman, to inherit with us who are free born?' Jephtha being thus treated in his native country, and being of a daring spirit, determined to try his fortune in a foreign one. He accordingly repaired to the land of Tob, where by his great courage and skill he soon raised himself to be the leader of a small army, with which he made excursions into the enemy's country, frequently returning laden with rich spoils. At that time the Ammonites made war with the Gileadites, invading them with a formidable army; and not content with ravaging their country, they threatened to lay siege to the city of Gilead itself. The Gileadites, on their part, raised a numerous army to oppose them, but were in great distress for want of an experienced general to lead their troops to battle. In this extremity, they thought of their country-man Jephtha, the fame of whose military exploits had by that time reached them. A deputation of the Elders repaired to that chieftain, humbly soliciting him to take command of their army. Jephtha was much surprised at this reverse of fortune, and said to the Elders: 'It was but the other day I was expelled my father's house, being deemed unworthy to inherit with the free born, but now in your distress you have recourse to me.' Recollecting it was his native country and his brethren (although unworthy) who were in distress, he told the Elders that if they would consent to make him their Chief General or Governor for life, in case he returned victorious from the Ammonitish expedition, he would accept their offer. To this they readily assented, and Jephtha's title was soon afterwards ratified in the city of Gilead, in a full assembly of the Chiefs and Elders. Jephtha being thus vested with full powers, reinforced the Gileaditish army with those veteran troops he had so successfully commanded; but being desirous, if possible, to spare the effusion of blood, he sent messages to the King of the Ammonites, requesting to know by what authority he invaded his country. That monarch haughtily answered 'That the country was not Jephtha's but his, for that the Israelites had taken it from his forefathers on their way from Egypt to Canaan, the land where the majority of the people then dwelt.' Jephtha replied, 'That it was not from the Ammonites, but the Amorites, the country had been taken, and that if the law of conquest or prescription could give a people proper title to a territory, the Gileadites had an undoubted one, having been in possession of theirs for 300 years.' The King of the Ammonites still continuing obstinate, Jephtha drew out his army in battle array, and marched against the invaders, who were totally defeated and put to flight with great slaughter. Following up their advantage, the Gileadites entered the enemy's territory, where their late ravages were severely retaliated by the plunder of twenty Ammonitish cities. On his return, Jephtha met with great molestation from his neighbours, the Ephriamites, who had crossed the River Jordan in a hostile manner, etc.

EXPLANATION OF THE THIRD DEGREE APRON

Bro .... by the WM's command, I invest you with the distinguishing badge of a MM *(attaches it)* to mark the further progress you have made in the science. Your white lambskin apron has been replaced by one with a light blue border, having three rosettes arranged in triangular fashion with the point uppermost. The colour of the silk, the triangle and the three rosettes, have special meanings. The two vertical ribbons; typify the pillars .... and .... the import of which has been explained to you. To each of these ribbons seven tassels are attached to remind us that no Lodge is perfect unless seven Brethren are present, that in olden days the seven ages of man were thought to be influenced by the seven then known planets, and no MM was considered efficient unless he had some knowledge of the seven liberal arts and sciences.

CHARGE AFTER RAISING

WM (*to Can*) — Brother, your zeal for the institution of Freemasonry, the progress which you have made in the art, and your conformity to the general regulations, have pointed you out as a proper object of our favour and esteem. In the character of a MM, you are henceforth authorised to correct the errors and irregularities of Brethren and Fellows, and guard them against a breach of fidelity. To improve the morals and correct the manners of men in society must be your constant care. With this view, therefore, you are always to recommend to inferiors obedience and submission; to equals, courtesy and affability; to superiors kindness and condescension. You are to inculcate universal benevolence, and, by the regularity of your own behaviour, afford the best example for the benefit of others. The Ancient Landmarks of the Order, which are here entrusted to your care, you are to preserve sacred and inviolable, and never suffer an infringement of our rites, or a deviation from established usage and custom. Duty, honour, and gratitude now bind you to be faithful to every trust, to support with becoming dignity your new character, and to enforce by example and precept the tenets of the system. Let no motive, therefore, make you swerve from your duty, violate your vows, or betray your trust; but be true and faithful, and imitate the example of that celebrated Artist whom you have once represented. By this exemplary conduct you will convince the world that merit has been your title to our privileges and that on you our favours have not been undeservedly bestowed.

ADDITIONAL ADDRESSES AT INSTALLATION

The Addresses set out in the Installation Ceremony in this book are those used at the Friday evening demonstrations at Emulation Lodge of Improvement, when not all officers permitted by the Constitutions are invested. Some Lodges find it helpful to have set forms of Address and the following are suggested.

ADDRESS TO CHAPLAIN.

WM *rises* — Bro ...., I appoint you Chaplain of the Lodge, and I now invest you with the Jewel of your office — *invests Chaplain with collar* — the Open Book. This represents the Volume of the Sacred Law, which is always open upon the Master's pedestal when the Brethren are at labour in the Lodge. The VSL is the greatest of the three great, though emblematical, lights in Freemasonry. The Sacred Writings are given as the rule and guide of our Faith. The Sacred Volume will guide us to all Truth, direct our steps in the paths of Happiness, and point out to us the whole Duty of man. Without it the Lodge is not perfect; and without an openly avowed belief in its Divine Author, no Candidate can be lawfully initiated into our Order. Your place in the Lodge is on the immediate left of the IPM, and as, both in the Opening and Closing of the Lodge in each Degree, as well as in each of the three Ceremonies, the Blessing of the Almighty is invoked on our proceedings, it will be your duty, as far as may be possible, to attend all the meetings of the Lodge, in order that you may exercise your sacred office in the devotional portions of our Ceremonies — *shakes hands with Chaplain and sits.*

ADDRESS TO DC AND ADC

WM *rises* — Bro ...., I appoint you DC of the Lodge, and I now invest you with the Collar and Jewel of your office — *invests DC or ADC with collar* — Your duty is to see that the ceremonies of the Lodge are carried on with propriety and decorum, the Visitors and Brethren, placed according to their rank and the officers in their respective stations. I trust you will give to your duties the attention which their importance demands — *shakes hands with DC or ADC and sits.*

ADDRESS TO THE CHARITY STEWARD.

With the creation of this additional office, another jewel has been added to the list of those with which a Master must invest his officers. In most cases of additional offices, the investiture by the Master should be in his own words without any formal 'ritual' piece to learn. However, there are already several such set ritual pieces prepared and being actively canvassed for use. In the additional office of Charity Steward, some Lodges use a piece which has been for many years included in some ritual books and is taken direct from the writings of William Preston, in his *Illustrations of Masonry*. It could be that, if Masters want some assistance on what to say, when investing the Charity Steward, they may also care to go back to

Preston's time with:

WM *rises* — Bro ...., I appoint you Charity Steward of the lodge and I now invest you with the jewel of your office — *invests Charity Steward with collar and jewel.* The Trowel teaches that nothing can be united without proper cement and that the perfection of a building must depend on the suitable disposition of that cement; so, Charity, the bond of perfection and social union, must link separate minds and separate interests, that, like the radii of a circle which extend from the centre to every part of the circumference, the principle of universal benevolence may be diffused to every member of the community.

ADDRESS TO ALMONER

There is no recognised form of address to the Almoner. The WM may invest this Officer with a few appropriate words.

ADDRESS TO ORGANIST

WM *rises* Bro ...., I appoint you Organist of the Lodge, and I now invest you with the Jewel of your office — *invests Organist with collar.* The Lyre is the emblem of Music, one of the seven liberal Arts and Sciences, the study of which is inculcated in the Fellow-Crafts' Degree. The records of Ancient History, both sacred and secular, testify that from the earliest times Music has borne a more or less important part in the celebration of religious rites and ceremonies; that Pagans and Monotheists, the Ancient Hebrews, and the more comparatively modern Christians have in all ages made full and free use of Music, as an aid to devotion, and in the expression of praise and thanksgiving in the services of their several systems of religion. In like manner Freemasonry, from the earliest period of its history, has availed itself of the aid of music in the performance of its rites and ceremonies: and we must all feel how much of impressiveness and solemnity is derived from the judicious introduction of instrumental music into those ceremonies. Music has been defined as 'the concord of sweet sounds'. In this aspect it typifies the concord and harmony which have always been among the foremost characteristics of our Order. Your Jewel, therefore, the emblem of Concord, should stimulate us to promote and to maintain concord, goodwill and affection, not only among the members of our own Lodge, but with all Brethren of the Craft — *shakes hands with organist and sits.*

ADDRESS TO STEWARDS

WM *rises* — Brothers ...... and ......, I appoint you stewards of the Lodge, and I now invest you with your Collars and Jewels of Office — *invests Stewards with collars* — Your duties are to introduce visitors, and see that they are properly accommodated, to assist in the collection of the dues and subscriptions, to keep an eye on the Lodge expenses at refreshment, and see that the tables are properly furnished and that every Brother is suitably provided for; and generally to assist the Ds and other officers in performing their respective duties. Your regular and early attendance will be the best proof of your zeal and attachment — *shakes hands with Stewards and sits.*

THE FOLLOWING ADDRESSES ARE USED BY SOME LODGES AS ALTERNATIVES

ALTERNATIVE ADDRESS TO IPM

WM — Bro ...., I invest you with the Jewel of IPM of this Lodge *(invests IPM with collar)* It is an office which is not in the power of the WM to bestow, being yours of right, as having faithfully performed your duty in the Craft. Your Jewel is the 47th Problem of the 1st Book of Euclid, which was one of the most important discoveries of the learned Brother Pythagoras; and in the joy of his heart he is said to have exclaimed *Eureka!* ('I have found it'), and to have sacrificed a hecatomb. As this figure depends upon several lines, angles, and triangles, which form the whole, so Freemasonry depends upon its several members, and the principles upon which the society is established. Some of our Brethren, from their station in life, standing as they do on the basis of earthly bliss, are emblematical of the great angle which subtends the right line; others, blessed with means to tread the flowery meads of prosperity and affluence, are descriptive of the squares which stand on the sides; those Brethren who enjoy every social comfort, and never exceed the bounds of mediocrity, symbolise the triangles within the square; and those who have the satisfaction of adminstering to the wants of the indigent and industrious may be compared to the triangle which surrounds and supports the figure; whilst the lines which form it may remind us of those Brethren who are incapable of providing the necessaries of life unless aided by cheerful and ready assistance.

ALTERNATIVE ADDRESS TO SW

WM — Bro ...., I appoint you SW of this Lodge, and I invest you with the Collar and Jewel of your office (*invests SW with collar*). The L being an emblem of equality, points out to you the equal measures you are bound to pursue, in conjunction with the Master, in the well ruling and governing of the Lodge. Your regular and punctual attendance at our stated meetings is essential and I rely upon your knowledge of Masonry, and your attachment to the Lodge, for the faithful discharge of the duties of your office. You will not fail to attend the Quarterly Communications of the Grand Lodge, in order that this Lodge may be properly represented. I give into your hands this Gavel *(hands Gavel to SW)*, as an emblem of power, which will enable you to preserve due order in the W. This Cn is the emblem of your office *(hands Cn to SW)*, and you will keep it in an erect position whilst the Brethren are at labour, as they are then under your superintendence; but place it in a horizontal position whilst at refreshment. I also intrust to your care this pillar of the Doric Order *(hands pillar to SW)*; it is an emblem of strength, and directs that you are to use all your strength of mind and powers of intellect to preserve peace, order and harmony among the Brethren of the

Lodge, facilitate the designs of the Master,
and see that his commands are carried into
full and permanent effect.

ALTERNATIVE ADDRESS TO JW

WM — Bro ...., I appoint you JW
of this Lodge, and I invest you with the
Collar and Jewel of your office *(invests JW
with collar)*. The P R, being an emblem of
uprightness, points out the integrity of the
measures you are bound to pursue in
conjunction with the Master and your
Brother SW, in the well ruling and governing of the Lodge; but more particularly to
that part of your duty which relates to the
admission of visitors, lest through your
neglect any unqualified person should gain
admission to our assemblies, and the
Brethren be thereby innocently led to
violate their Obl. You are to be regular in
your attendance at our stated meetings, to
assist in transacting the business of the
evening; this is necessary, as unless due
attention be paid by the officers, you
cannot expect the Brethren to be punctual
at the appointed time. I now place in your

hand this Gavel *(hands Gavel to JW)*, as an emblem of power, to enable you to preserve due order in the S. This Cn is the emblem of your office *(hands Cn to JW)*, and you will keep it in an erect position whilst at refreshment, as the Brethren are then under your superintendence; but place it horizontally whilst at labour. I likewise intrust to your care this pillar of the Corinthian Order *(hands pillar to JW)*, which is an emblem of beauty, and points out that you are to adorn the work with all your powers of genius and active industry, and promote regularity amongst the Brethren by your good example, the persuasive eloquence of precept, and the administrative encouragement of merit.

ADDITION TO ADDRESS TO TREASURER

WM — Bro ...., you have been elected Treasurer of the Lodge, I now invest you with the insignia of your office *(invests Treasurer with collar)*, which is a key appended to a collar. Your duty is to receive all fees, dues, etc, except those which are required to be transmitted to the

GS for registrations, certificates, and the fund of Benevolence, which must be deposited in the hands of the WM, who is responsible for their legal appropriation. You are to pay from the Lodge funds all current expenses, also any sums which may be voted by the Brethren for the purposes of charity. Your accounts must be fairly entered in a book which should be opened at every meeting of the Lodge that the members may know how their subscriptions have been applied and how the balance stands. I feel assured that your regard for the fraternity will prompt you to the faithful discharge of the duties of your office.

ADDITION TO ADDRESS TO SECRETARY

WM — Bro ...., I appoint you Secretary of the Lodge, and I now invest you with the Jewel of your office (*invests Secretary with collar*), which is two pens in saltire. It is your duty to issue the summons, detailing all matters of business which may be brought forward in the Lodge, to attend the Lodge punctually, and to enter the proceedings in the minutes, for confirmation at a subsequent regular meeting of the Lodge. It is required that you should keep a correct register of the names and addresses of all the members, and make the legal returns to the Grand Lodge. You must also keep a true account of the payment of all fees, dues, and subscriptions, giving notice to every member who is in arrears. Your inclination and zeal for Freemasonry will, I doubt not, induce you to discharge the duties of your office with fidelity, so as to merit the confidence and esteem of the Brethren.

ALTERNATIVE ADDRESS TO THE CHARITY STEWARD

WM — *rises* — Bro ......, I appoint you Charity Steward of the Lodge and I now invest you with the Jewel of your office which is a Trowel. You are to put your hand to the Trowel of peace and beneficence and not lay it by so long as you are able to join one stone to the building. Beneficence, or active goodness, is the perfection of that goodwill we owe to mankind; and remember that the Almighty has laid this injunction upon us, that we should not withhold our hand when it is in our power to do good. Let the poor and indigent be assisted. The advantages arising from a conscientious discharge of this duty are great and many; and when we communicate happiness to another, and with a good heart, that happiness is directly returned back to us.

ADDRESS ON PRESENTATION OF THE HALL-STONE JEWEL

(The following Address may be used by the IM when transferring the Hall-Stone Lodge Collarette and Jewel to his successor at the Installation Meeting immediately before the investiture of officers.*)

IM *displays the Jewel to WM* — Worshipful Master I now present to your notice the Hall-Stone Jewel, which was conferred on this Lodge by the Most Worshipful Grand Master. You will observe that its form is symbolic, for on the side squares are inscribed the dates 1914-1918; four years of supreme sacrifice. In the centre is a winged figure, representing Peace, supporting a Temple. This symbolises the gift made by the English Craft of a new Temple in memory of those Brethren who made the supreme sacrifice in the cause of their King and their country.

The Jewel is suspended by the Square and Compasses, two of the Great though

*See *Notes on Ritual and Procedure*

Emblematical Lights in Freemasonry, and is attached to a ribbon, which I now have much pleasure in placing about your neck. *(WM rises and IM adjusts the Collarette, after which WM resumes his seat.)*

IM — The wearing of that Jewel by the Master of a Lodge fulfils a double purpose. First, it provides visible evidence that the Lodge has faithfully and conscientiously discharged its obligations to the Fraternity; secondly, it should ever provide an inspiration to every Brother to put service before self.

That Jewel, which should always by worn as part of your Masonic clothing Worshipful Master, you will transfer to your successor on the occasion when he is installed in the high and honourable Office which you now occupy. He, in turn, will transfer it to his successor, and so it is to be hoped, it will ever adorn the Master of this Lodge, until time with us shall be no more.

THE PRESENTATION OF A
GRAND LODGE CERTIFICATE

There is no formal ritual for the presentation to a Master Mason of his Grand Lodge Certificate but many Lodges prefer that some formality be observed in the presentation and the attention of the recipient drawn to the significance of the document and the nature of its design. Several forms are in general use and that printed below which has been extensively used by Bro O. C. Klagge PJGD, is suggested as appropriate in its following the Masonic Lectures in dealing with those parts of the Certificate which are similar in design to the First Degree Tracing Board in its representation of the Lodge and its Furniture, Ornaments and Jewels.

Attention is also drawn to the Recommendations adopted by Grand Lodge on points of procedure in which that relating to attendance at Lodges overseas recommends that on the presentation to a Master Mason of his Grand Lodge

Certificate he should be warned not to make any Masonic contacts overseas with members of other Jurisdictions without having ascertained by application to the Grand Secretary the existence of regular Masonry in the country concerned, and the address to which Masonic enquiries in that country should be directed.

ADDRESS

As a Master mason you are entitled to receive from Grand Lodge a certificate stating that you have been regularly initiated, passed and raised.

I now present to you your certificate, and if you will examine it I shall give an explanation of its significance and some of its symbolism. The certificate is headed by the Arms of the Grand Master, an item which naturally changes with the change of Grand Master, but the rest of the design of the certificate depicting various masonic emblems has remained unaltered since first introduced in 1819. These emblems represent ornaments, furniture or appointments in a Lodge of Freemasons and taken together may be regarded as a pictorial representation of a Lodge. Apart from one item these emblems are all described in the Lecture on the First Degree and so appear with others on the First Degree Tracing Board which was devised to illustrate the First Lecture, so that the certificate may be regarded as a simplified First Degree Tracing Board.

The outstanding feature on the certificate is the representation of the three great Pillars. These pillars are said to support a Freemason's Lodge; that in the centre is of the Ionic Order, that on the left of the Doric Order and that on the right of the Corinthian Order. In Masonry they are called Wisdom, Strength and Beauty and represent Solomon, King of Israel, for his Wisdom in building, completing and dedicating the Temple at Jerusalem to God's service, Hiram King of Tyre for his Strength in supporting him with men and materials, and Hiram Abif for his curious and masterly workmanship in beautifying and adorning the same. These pillars are physically represented in the Lodge by the candlesticks supporting the three lesser lights, that by the Master being of the Ionic Order denoting Wisdom, that by the SW is of the Doric Order denoting Strength, and that by the JW of the Corinthian Order denoting Beauty.

These pillars rest on the Black and White Mosaic or chequered pavement of the Lodge representing the Light and Darkness, the joys and sorrows of our chequered existence on this earth. On the Mosaic pavement are seen the Celestial and Terrestrial Globes, pointing out Masonry universa!. This is the item not described in the First Lecture and so does not appear on the First Tracing Board. The Globes were originally a regular feature in a lodge, but have now largely disappeared as normal furniture. They are sometimes seen on the tops of pillars in the West of a Lodge, and small representations of the globes are frequently seen on the tops of the Warden's columns.

There is also depicted what in the Lecture is called the furniture of the Lodge, the VSL, Square and Compasses, also referred to as the three great though emblematical Lights. The three great Lights displayed on the Master's pedestal are usually depicted together, but here the compasses are shown elsewhere.

There are further depicted what are described as Jewels, three movable and three immovable. The Movable Jewels are the square, level and plumb-rule. They are called jewels on account of their moral tendency, as the square teaches morality, the level equality and the plumb-rule justness and uprightness of life and actions. They are called Movable Jewels because they are worn by the Master and his Wardens and are transferable to their successors on nights of Installation. The Immovable Jewels are the Tracing Board, the Rough and Perfect Ashlars. They are called Immovable Jewels because they lie open and immovable in the Lodge for the Brethren to moralise on.

The Tracing Board is for the Master to lay lines and draw designs on, the Rough Ashlar for the entered apprentice to work, mark and indent on, and the Perfect Ashlar for the experienced craftsman to try and adjust his jewels on. The Tracing Board depicted here and on the First Degree Tracing Board, is a true tracing, draughtsman's or drawing board, and as a draughtsman requires a rule and pencil to assist him to lay lines and draw designs, a ruler and pencil are shown as necessary accessories to the Tracing Board. The Rough Ashlar is described as a stone, rough and unhewn, as taken from the quarry, and as the entered apprentice requires a chisel and Mason's maul to render the Rough Ashlar fit for the intended structure, these implements are shown as necessary accessories to the Rough Ashlar. The Perfect Ashlar is described as a stone of a true die or square, fit only to be tried by the square and compasses. The square is already shown in front of the VSL, so the Compasses alone are shown as a necessary accessory to the Perfect Ashlar, required to test its trueness.

Until comparatively recently the left hand space between the Pillars stated in English that the Brother named had been

rother below that rank presides, *i*
..†

hen the Ceremony is for Opening o
ing a Provincial or District Granc
e, the Lodge is so described and the
of the appropriate Provincial o
ct Grand Officers substituted for
of Grand Lodge. In accordance with
79 of the Book of Constitutions when
rovincial or District Grand Master
es in a Provincial or District Grand
, it is to be declared opened or closed
form; in all other cases, *in form*.†

GM *one* ➙ ⚊ **SGW** *one* ➙ ⚊
ne ➙ ⚊.

GM — Brethren, assist me to open
*se)*this Grand Lodge.

rise.

GM — Brother Grand Pursuivant,
your situation in Grand Lodge?

– Within the Inner Porch of Grand
MWGM.

M — What is your duty?

– To give a due report of all
ing Brethren, and to see that they
rly clothed and ranged under their

regularly initiated, passed and raised, and a translation into Latin appeared in the right hand space, but the declaration is now made only in English. The year of Initiation is, however, shown as AL, that is Anno Lucis, or the year in the era of Masonic Light which precedes the Christian era by four thousand years.

The seal of Grand Lodge has been impressed, and the certificate is signed by the Grand Secretary.

Your certificate is a sort of passport to regular freemasonry, and as you may be asked to produce it when visiting a Lodge in a foreign constitution recognised by Grand Lodge, or even a Lodge in this country where you are not known, it is advisable to keep it handy with your regalia. It should not, therefore, be framed and hung in your office or even in your home.

The certificate, however, states that the production of the certificate itself does not entitle you to admission to a Lodge without examination.

Your certificate is not yet complete as it

requires your usual signature in the place
provided in the margin, and from which
there should be no future variation. This
you will now append at the Secretary's
table.

a E
form
W
Clos
Lodg
titles
Distr
those
Rule
the P
presid
Lodge
in due
MW
JGW
MW
(or clos
ALL
MWG
where is
GP —
Lodge,
MWG
GP —
approach
are prope

THE OPENING AND CL
GRAND LODGE A
PROVINCIAL AND I
GRAND LODG

The same form of Open
Ceremonies are used for C
for Provincial and Distric
The only difference betw
and Closing Ceremonies
of the appropriate word
Prayer is used.

The Ceremony follo
occasions when Gran
and closed by the M
Ceremony is condu
qualified Brother, the
substituted where ne
noted that in accord
the Book of Consti
Grand Master or
Assistant Grand Ma
Lodge, it is declare
due form and not in

J

respective banners.

MWGM — Do you find them so placed?

GP — To the best of my knowledge, MWGM.

MWGM — Where is the situation of the JGW?

GP — In the South, MWGM.

MWGM — Brother JGW, whom do you represent?

JGW — ...., prince of the people, on Mount Tabor.

MWGM — Where is the situation of the SGW?

JGW — In the West, MWGM.

MWGM — Brother SGW, whom do you represent?

SGW — ...., the Assistant High Priest, on Mount Sinai.

MWGM — Where is the situation of the Deputy GM?

SGW — At the right of the MWGM.

MWGM — Brother DGM, whom do you represent?

DGM — HA, the Prince of Architects.

MWGM — What is your duty?

DGM — To lay schemes, draw designs and assist the MWGM in the execution of the work.

MWGM — Where is the situation of the MWGM?

DGM — In the East.

MWGM — Whom does he represent?

DGM — The Royal Solomon.

MWGM — Brethren, I call on the Grand Chaplain to invoke the blessing of the G A O T U.

For Opening

G Chap — G A O T U, without Whose special and preventing grace all human efforts are of no avail, mercifully hear our supplications and grant that our labours, thus begun in order and obedience to our Laws, may please Thee both in will and deed and evermore redound to the honour of Thy Holy Name.

ALL — S M I B.

MWGM — In the name of the Royal Solomon, I declare this Grand Lodge opened in ample form† — *one* ▬♦.

SGW — *One* ▬♦ *and raises column.*

JGW — *One* ▬♦ *and lowers column.*

For Closing

G Chap — Accept we beseech Thee, G A O T U, our humble and hearty thanks for the many blessings we derive from Thine infinite Goodness. Grant that the precepts and principles of the Order may be deeply engraven on our hearts and so dispose our words and actions, that eschewing those things that are contrary to our profession, and following all such things as are agreeable to the same, they may continue to cement and adorn the Sacred Edifice both now and evermore.

ALL — S M I B.

MWGM — In the name of the Royal Solomon I declare this Grand Lodge closed in ample form† — *one* ⬛.

SGW — *one* ⬛ *and lowers column.*
JGW — *one* ⬛ *and raises column.*

(In Grand Lodge the VSL and the S and Cs are attended to by the GDC).

Symbolism in Craft Freemasonry

Colin F. W. Dyer

Freemasonry, in its lodges and ceremonies, makes use of a great deal of symbolism, the origin of the great majority of which is open to speculation. Freemasons of earlier times have not left precise records giving the definite origins of most of the symbols they brought into use in the Craft. Many parallel instances of the use of symbols may be found by which it is possible that freemasonry could have been influenced, while masonic symbolism has been a favourite subject for writers in the past.

In this book the author has examined a great deal of material in endeavouring to establish the reasons for the incorporation of particular symbolism into masonry. Colin Dyer is well known for his research into masonic history and is the author of several books on masonic subjects. The reader's knowledge and appreciation of masonic symbolism cannot fail to be enhanced by reading this important new book.

LEWIS MASONIC